Reading Aloud and Beyond

Reading Aloud and Beyond

Fostering the Intellectual Life with Older Readers

FRANK SERAFINI

CYNDI GIORGIS

HEINEMANN
Portsmouth, NH

Heinemann
A division of Reed Elsevier Inc.
361 Hanover Street
Portsmouth, NH 03801–3912
www.heinemann.com

Offices and agents throughout the world

Library of Congress Cataloging-in-Publication Data
Serafini, Frank.
  Reading aloud and beyond : fostering the intellectual life with older readers /
    Frank Serafini, Cyndi Giorgis.
       p. cm.
  Includes bibliographical references.
  ISBN 0-325-00522-2
  1. Oral reading—Handbooks, manuals, etc. 2. Reading (Elementary)—Hand-
  books, manuals, etc. 3. School children—Books and reading—Handbooks,
  manuals, etc. I. Giorgis, Cyndi. II. Title.
LB1573.5.S47 2003
372.45'2—dc21   2003007498

Editor: Lois Bridges
Production: Elizabeth Valway
Cover design and illustration: Jenny Jensen Greenleaf
Composition: GEX Publishing Services
Manufacturing: Steve Bernier

Printed in the United States of America on acid-free paper
07 06 05 04 03 VP 1 2 3 4 5

This book is dedicated to the memory of our fathers,
Frank William Serafini Sr.
and
Glenn E. Martens,
who instilled in us a lifelong love of reading.

Contents

CONTENTS

Acknowledgments

We would like to acknowledge our mothers, Dolores Serafini (Frank's mom) and Donna Zanetti (Cyndi's mom), and our families for all of their love and caring throughout the years.

Our department chair, Dr. Greg Levitt, has provided and continues to provide support for our numerous endeavors, academic and otherwise. The esteemed faculty in the Department of Curriculum and Instruction—you know who you are—continue to challenge our ideas and strengthen our commitment to education. We thank you.

Our graduate assistants, Tracy and Christina, helped us pull books, make copies, and maintain our sanity throughout this process.

Our favorite authors and illustrators, mentioned throughout the pages of this book, make reading aloud worthwhile.

Our favorite editor, Lois Bridges, makes working with her a pleasure. Her kind words helped us believe in ourselves as writers.

Finally, Sharon and Jim, our best friends and companions, put up with late hours, bizarre conversations, and whining. You still love us and we love you for that.

Introduction

And, of course, the best way to cultivate their [children's] taste is to read to them, starting at birth and keeping on and on. "Let me hear you read it" is a test. "Let me read it to you" is a gift.

KATHERINE PATERSON
The Spying Heart

When we think back to the most powerful experiences in our literate lives, we think of being read to. Whether it was a teacher, a parent, a sibling, or a distant relative who read to us, we remember the feelings of comfort and the sense of adventure in losing ourselves in a good story. At times, the book was simply a prop; what mattered most was the sense of belonging, the feelings of being loved. It took time for us to realize that the story was just as important as the sense of caring that developed around literature. We connected those wonderful stories to those caring individuals with whom we experienced literature, and then we connected to the stories themselves.

Several books have been written to help teachers learn how to effectively read aloud in their classrooms; so has this one. Books have been written explaining the benefits of reading aloud and advocating this practice across grade levels; so has this one. Books have also been written that provide bibliographies for teachers to refer to when selecting appropriate literature for reading aloud; so has this one.

But rather than viewing reading aloud simply as an instructional strategy designed to enhance the curriculum, *Reading Aloud and Beyond* envisions the read aloud as the foundation of the reading curriculum, the launching point for the study of the language arts and the content area disciplines. We don't just read books that go along with our units of study, we read books that *construct* our units of study. Literature, be it fictional stories or informational text, provides experiences for understanding the world that other resources cannot. It is a way of knowing. We want teachers to appreciate the unique qualities of literature and its fundamental role in the curriculum, not simply to regard it as an appendage to hang onto an existing curriculum.

Our goal is to introduce intermediate elementary and middle school teachers to the joys and benefits of sharing quality picture books, chapter books, informational texts, and poetry with older readers through the read-aloud experience. We want teachers to appreciate these works of literature in and of themselves, before using them to teach reading skills and strategies. In other words, we believe that you should love the literature you read before you share it with your students. This book makes a case for reading aloud as the foundation of the reading and content area curriculum, as an essential component of the reading instructional framework. It is a lens through which to see the world, not simply a mirror to reflect a particular study or curriculum.

Time allotted for reading aloud in the intermediate elementary and middle school classroom has been pushed to the periphery of the reading and language arts curriculum by mandated commercial literacy programs and by an increasing demand from public stakeholders for higher standardized test scores. In response to this pressure, we provide sound theoretical and research-based arguments for spending valuable class time reading aloud with children. In this book we argue for the importance of creating effective interpretive communities in intermediate- and middle-grade classrooms and establish a basis for developing literacy lessons that utilize quality picture and chapter books during classroom reading aloud experiences.

Various chapters address in detail how to go about reading books aloud and facilitating quality discussions that focus on the literature being read. We have come to call these interactions "invested discussions" and include numerous examples and suggestions for developing student investment in literature discussions. Each of these strategies is designed to help classroom teachers engage students in the books they read and extend their discussions beyond the "I Like It" phase.

Along with providing a quick overview of the research that supports reading literature aloud with older readers, this book is designed to be a practical handbook for busy teachers. It is filled with instructional suggestions for teachers and examples of learning experiences we have used and found to be effective in our classrooms and the classrooms of the teachers with whom we work. The learning experiences we describe contain useful guidelines for teachers attempting to build their literacy curriculum on the foundation of reading aloud with students. Our instructional strategies are flexible enough that you can adapt them to fit your own classroom schedule and instructional style.

Reading Aloud and Beyond includes suggestions about sharing chapter books and informational texts but focuses on the use of picture books. We believe that the length and format of the picture book make it a perfect resource, one that often goes untapped in the intermediate and middle grades. For this reason, we focus on weaving picture books throughout the curriculum.

It is our hope that this book will never sit on your classroom shelf. We would love to see dog-eared copies of *Reading Aloud and Beyond* on the classroom floor near a read aloud chair or on the school librarian's desk. Our goal is to help teachers extend their use of the read aloud experience on a daily basis and to provide additional support as teachers try new instructional strategies across the curriculum.

Reading Aloud and Beyond is divided into two parts. Part I, Chapters 1–5, talks about what happens before the actual read aloud experience begins; how the actual read aloud experience looks in practice; how to carefully select quality pieces of literature; how to think about their possible curricular connections; how to analyze the illustrations and text in the books chosen; and how to design opportunities for students to engage in more sophisticated discussions.

In Part II, Chapters 6–12, we share ideas about what we do during and after reading a piece of literature aloud with our students. We describe in detail how to promote invested discussions; extend the read aloud experience to support curricular connections; provide opportunities to respond to our read alouds; and assess students' understandings of the literature we share. We include appendices, and our favorite read aloud picture books, chapter books, authors, and illustrators.

Daniel Pennac opened his book *Better Than Life* by saying, "You can't make people read. Any more than you can make them love, or dream" (1999). We agree with him. The best we can do is create a space where readers are invited into the world of literature, are read with every day, are encouraged to talk openly about their ideas and feelings concerning literature, are supported by knowledgeable others, and have access to a wealth of reading materials to use and take home to share. *Reading Aloud and Beyond* provides a foundation on which teachers can build their literacy curriculum, connecting authors, illustrators, and readers in a mutually satisfying relationship. It is with these goals in mind that we begin this book.

This book is grounded in the following theoretical principles:

1. Authentic literature should play a prominent role in the elementary curriculum.

2. Reading literature aloud with students creates collaborative, literate communities of readers that support individual literacy development.

3. Literature should be honored in and of itself, not just as a vehicle for literacy and content area instruction.

4. The sharing of authentic children's literature fosters the development of critical thinking, cultural awareness, and democratic principles, and prepares children to live in a diverse society.

5. Understandings are developed in the social context of literature discussions, where the teacher's role is to extend students' learning and responses to literature rather than simply to evaluate their answers.

6. The choices teachers make concerning the literature they read affects the quality of the students' discussions and responses.

7. Being able to read aloud eloquently and effectively takes practice.

8. Read alouds—and the discussions that occur before, during, and after read alouds—provide the foundation for the elementary literacy curriculum.

9. Teachers use read alouds to inspire readers to read; to investigate new authors, genres, illustrators, and topics; and to introduce readers to works of literature that they may not find on their own.

10. Literature not only provides the foundation for the reading and language arts curriculum, but provides the basis for all content area instruction as well.

Figure I–1. Theoretical Foundations

Reading Aloud and Beyond

1

The Read Aloud as Experience

Every experience takes up something from those [experiences]
that have come before and modifies in some way the quality
of those which come after.

JOHN DEWEY
Experience and Education

The research evidence is irrefutable. Common sense tells us it must be so. Classroom observations and experiences confirm our deeply held beliefs and intuitions. Namely, reading aloud with children supports their development as readers and writers, fosters their love of reading, improves reading skills and abilities, encourages them to continue reading throughout their lives, and, yes, even increases their achievement on standardized tests. Yet the majority of the professional resources concerning reading aloud focus on the primary grades—kindergarten through third. What happens in the intermediate elementary and middle school grades? Reading aloud is just as important for older readers as it is for younger ones and should occur every day, into the intermediate-grade classrooms and beyond.

We believe that reading aloud is more than an instructional strategy, a nice break in the day, or a device to calm students down after recess. We believe that the read aloud experience is the foundation for the language arts and content area curriculum. It is an experience involving different elements; namely, a teacher or reader, a group of students, and a piece of literature, that come together to create a coherent whole.

As you may have noticed, we have been using, and will continue to use, the phrase "reading *with* children," instead of the more familiar phrase, "reading *to* children." We have done this for very specific reasons. The phrase, "reading aloud *to* children" projects an image of teachers, students, and literature as separate entities, where teachers stand apart from students, reading "at" them, then requiring them to respond back to the teacher. This is not how we envision the read aloud experience.

By "reading *with* children," we envision a unified literacy event, a synthesis of teacher, literature, and students that constructs meanings and shares interpretations. Aligning with the work of Louise Rosenblatt, we conceptualize reading literature aloud as a specific experience, a unique event at a particular time and place, in which each element—teacher, students, texts, and social contexts (both immediate context and larger, sociocultural context)—conditions the other and is part of a unique transaction. Rather than viewing each of these elements as separate entities, we, like Rosenblatt and Dewey, see them as a comprehensive experience. They cannot be understood separately. Take the text, the teacher, or the students away and it is no longer a read aloud experience. Further, each read aloud experience is a unique event that builds upon the experiences that have come before it and supports the experiences with literature that follow.

In our community of readers, our definition of what it means to read and be a reader is created by the way we read aloud with our students, the literature we choose to share, the demonstrations we provide as readers, the expectations we have for how our students respond to their readings, and the ways in which we encourage students to represent their understandings of the stories we read. In other words, we construct what it means to read, to make meanings with texts, and to be a successful reader in the context of our classroom by what we choose to attend to and by the expectations we set for our students.

As classroom teachers and university professors, we don't see ourselves standing apart from our students; rather, we see ourselves as fellow members of a community of readers, sharing favorite pieces of literature and responses with each other. We are simply the voice through which the book, the language, and the ideas of the author are brought to life. We listen to the stories that we read so that we can participate in the discussion alongside our students, not in front of them.

The Role of Literature in the Reading Curriculum

When people use the term "literature-based reading instruction," they generally do not mean that literature will become the foundation for the entire curriculum. They usually mean that teachers need to go out and find some picture books that fit in with their unit on dinosaurs or bears and read a few of these during the unit. Instead of this superficial connection between literature and the curriculum, we believe that the literature we read and the experiences we construct around literature *generate* the curriculum. Literature is not an added attraction designed to motivate reluctant readers; it is the driving force behind the curriculum we construct with our students.

Many contemporary commercial reading programs push literature to the periphery of the reading curriculum. Some use literature as a bonus, something to be read when one's "reading work" is completed. Others see books as "reading trophies," something to be collected like stars along a chart hung on the classroom wall. These programs seem more concerned with accumulating points and extrinsic rewards than with the aesthetic experience that accompanies reading literature. Utilizing computer-based reading tests, these programs focus on information that can be regurgitated quickly, calling this process "comprehension." We don't align with any of these beliefs.

Through the read aloud experience, we don't just teach a unit in social studies and make connections to a few read alouds during the reading workshop. We don't use computerized quizzes to assess reader ability to memorize "facts" from a text. The literature shared during the read aloud experience provides a place from which our curriculum can emerge. The experiences shared during the read aloud are not simply "connected" to the social studies unit, they become the foundation for the social studies unit. Through the read aloud experience, we are able to demonstrate the literate abilities we want to develop in our students, provide examples of the interactions and responses to literature we expect in our classrooms, and help students find new ways of understanding the various topics in the content areas. Literature is used as a lens to understand the world and becomes the launching point for our curriculum.

For example, we do not look for good books to read aloud simply because they fit with our unit on the Civil War, although we know many that would align with this topic. We read aloud carefully selected books that focus on the Civil War because they provide a unique way of understanding the Civil War, the events that took place, the people involved, and the issues that were important during that time in our history. Literature brings as much knowledge and understanding to our curriculum as do the reference materials we choose to include in our study. In fact, many of the learning experiences we create during a particular unit of study emerge from reading and sharing picture and chapter books, without referencing textbooks at all.

In *The Reading Workshop: Creating Space for Readers* (2001), Frank described a unit of study in the language arts/reading curriculum on the theme Escaping Reality. The picture books that were read and shared were the foundation of the unit of study. Each day as his class read a new picture book, beginning with *Where the Wild Things Are* by Maurice Sendak and progressing through a series of specially selected pieces of literature, the connections made, the impressions constructed, the questions asked, and the direction the study took all were based on the literature shared during the read aloud experience. Although Frank had predetermined the theme and selected a majority of the books to be read, the unit of study, the actual curriculum, was constructed *with* his students as they explored the elements of fantasy and reality represented in the various books. The books weren't connected to the study, they *were* the study.

The Role of the Teacher

The metaphor "teacher as docent," meaning "one who guides a tour," comes close to what we see as the role of the classroom teacher during the read aloud experience. Museum docents take visitors on tours of a museum helping them understand what it is they are seeing, offering interpretations concerning the art on display, and helping museum patrons come to new understandings about the artifacts they are experiencing. In much the same way, the teacher-docent helps literary "visitors" make meaning in transaction with the literary artifacts they have heard read aloud and helps them engage at a deeper level than they could on their own.

On the one hand, the classroom teacher needs to be extremely knowledgeable about children's literature and literary theory and how to facilitate a classroom discussion. Knowledge of children's literature helps teachers understand what is possible, what the piece of literature brings to the read aloud experience. At the same time, knowledge of one's students enables teachers to take the classroom discussion to new levels and to support students' insights and interpretations of the stories being shared. Knowing children's literature, knowing your students, and knowing how to facilitate classroom discussions strengthens the read aloud experience. It is this blend of knowledge and abilities that makes for effective teacher-docents.

As teachers, it is our role to help illuminate the texts we read, expanding their possibilities by helping students construct new and varied interpretations of them. Our goal is not to guide students to reach consensus or reduce their experiences with literature to the discovery of single, correct main ideas. Rather, we want to help them construct interpretations from a variety of perspectives and be able to make connections between the literature read and events in their lives. It is our job to help each child see literature, and the world, with new eyes.

As docents, we teach *into* children's learning as well as in front of it. We plan experiences ahead of time, but we are always cognizant of the opportunities presented during the reading event to take advantage of the teachable moment. In order to do so, we must remove ourselves from the front of the room and stop directing every movement. We have to learn to walk alongside our students, as docents, to help them explore the literature they read and the experiences they encounter.

4

The Role of the Student

It is our hope that every student will be engaged in every story we read aloud. We know this doesn't always happen, but it is our hope. The more they are engaged in the literature we read, the more interesting their responses and discussions will become. By engagement, we don't necessarily mean students have to enjoy every piece of literature we select to read aloud. We have had some tremendous discussions based on students' dislikes and on books they found boring or offensive. As long as there is some reaction to the stories we choose, positive or negative, we have a good chance of having an engaging discussion.

Before our students can engage with the literature we choose to read aloud, they need to become effective listeners. They need to be able to sustain the story in their minds and pay close attention to the illustrations when they are made available. Listening to the story and paying close attention to the illustrations provides the impetus for students' interpretations and discussions. Becoming a better listener is the foundation of our community of readers and our classroom discussions.

Students have to understand that they are expected to generate interpretations and share these with their classmates. In order to do so, they need to feel comfortable sharing their ideas, even those that are "half-formed." Students begin to feel comfortable when their ideas are respected and listened to by other students. Developing a community of readers helps support this type of interactions. We will discuss this more in Chapter 5.

Finding a Place in the Reading Curriculum

Reading aloud quality literature with children develops listening and reading skills, increases students' vocabulary, develops an appreciation of stories and written language, and expands students' ability to respond to literature. The importance of reading aloud with older readers may be common knowledge in some corners of the teaching profession; however, many classroom teachers need to articulate their reasons for doing so and offer research studies to support their decision to spend valuable time reading aloud with children. In today's public school settings time is at a premium, and only those literacy experiences that have been proven to be successful will be allowed to remain. Therefore, teachers need to understand the research evidence and theories necessary to defend their read aloud practices to parents, administrators, and, possibly, state legislators. We want teachers to respect the literature they read enough to weave it throughout their studies, not just add it on when they find a book that fits. It is toward this goal that we continue our story.

2

13 Good (Scientifically Based) Reasons to Read Aloud with Older Readers

The problem is that we teachers are hurried usurers, lending out the knowledge we possess and charging interest. It has to show a profit, and the quicker the better! If not, we might start losing faith in our own methods.

DANIEL PENNAC
Better Than Life

In contemporary society, if things don't happen quickly, we see a need to change them, to hurry them along. Fast-food restaurants, drive-up dry cleaners, and convenience stores have thrived on the basis of providing fast, if not necessarily quality, service. In public education, if current school reform efforts don't show measurable gains on standardized tests in a matter of minutes, they are often discarded in the fervor to locate the next "silver bullet" reading program that will solve the literacy crisis, engage all students, calm the nerves of concerned parents, raise standardized test scores, and win someone the next school board election.

In the opening quote, Pennac refers to the need for teaching methods to show a profit quickly or else face elimination. In today's political climate, profit equates with increased test scores. Although we believe—and scientifically based research supports our belief—that reading aloud with children increases tests scores, it is not the sole reason we read aloud with children.

A variety of research studies indicate that the predominance of reading aloud occurs in the primary grades, rather than in intermediate, middle, or high school classrooms. These same studies also suggest that picture books are rarely used beyond the third grade. Unfortunately, in many traditionally oriented classrooms reading aloud, when it is used, is often seen as a way of controlling children or calming them down after recess, rather than as an important reading instructional strategy.

Many classroom teachers have long viewed reading aloud as a luxury, an added expense that can be cut from the classroom "budget" in order to make room for more important instructional activities in the already overcrowded reading curriculum. As students progress through the elementary grades, they encounter fewer and fewer opportunities to hear stories, to see demonstrations of reading aloud, to talk about what has been read aloud, and to enjoy literature with their fellow classmates.

Activities designed to mimic standardized test experiences are being forced upon students with greater and greater tenacity. Because of the pressure from federal and state legislatures to raise test scores, public school classrooms may become places where children learn to read well enough to score higher on standardized tests, but may not be places where you learn to love to read, discover great authors and pieces of literature, or learn how to read in order to succeed in the "real" world. If we make reading in schools so boring, so sanitized, that children refuse to engage in reading have we, in fact, educated them at all? Reading instruction in schools should develop students' passion to read, support their engagements with texts of all sorts, and encourage them to become lifelong readers capable of fully participating in a democratic society.

In order to ensure that teacher candidates (preservice, education students) come to see the value in reading aloud and learn strategies for incorporating reading aloud into their curriculum once they have a class of their own, we need to expose them to reading aloud and literature discussions in their university coursework. If college professors do not demonstrate the importance of reading aloud, if they do not support teacher candidates as they practice this important instructional strategy and explain how to use read alouds as the foundation for reading instruction, chances are that teacher candidates will not value these learning experiences once they become certified teachers themselves.

Unfortunately—or fortunately if you are so inclined—one way to defend the practice of reading aloud with children is to cite research to suggest that reading aloud increases achievement on standardized tests, such as *Becoming a Nation of Readers* (Anderson et al. 1985). This may be the only way to prove to some legislators, parents, and school administrators that reading aloud should be part of every reading instructional framework. We, however, have come up with a list of thirteen good, scientifically based reasons for reading aloud that goes well beyond increased achievement on standardized tests as a rationale for this particular classroom experience. Increased test scores may be a fortunate, though indirect, consequence of reading aloud, but it should not drive every instructional and curricular decision we make. Our list includes thirteen reasons for reading aloud with children, in particular older readers; there are probably many other reasons you can think of, too.

Reason Number 1: Reading aloud increases test scores. Since administrators, school board members, legislators, and the United States Department of Education often rely on increased standardized test scores to defend particular classroom learning experiences and instructional practices, we begin by reiterating that scientifically based reading research shows that reading aloud with older readers increases achievement on standardized test scores and helps develop students' reading abilities. The Commission on Reading concluded, "the single most important activity for building the knowledge required for eventual success is reading aloud to children" (Anderson et al. 1985, 23). Reading aloud increases students' background knowledge, introduces them to various story structures, and demonstrates competent reading strategies—all of which contribute to increased reading ability and achievement on standardized tests.

Reason Number 2: Reading aloud introduces readers to new titles, authors, illustrators, genres, and text structures. Young readers often do not know what is available in the world of literature, and so it is up to us as classroom teachers, teacher educators, and school librarians to help them discover new literary treasures. With the plethora of new titles available today, and the vast array of classic children's literature in most school libraries, we are able to expose students to a variety of genres, structures, authors, and illustrators. The easiest way to do this is by reading aloud to them several times each day. We want to help students make connections with authors and story characters, become invested in the books they read, gain an appetite for literature, and develop into lifelong readers.

Children often choose to reread the books we read aloud to them. It is for this reason we need to be careful when selecting literature to share with students. There are so many wonderful titles available to choose from, however, in a range of genres and structures, that classroom teachers should have more problems narrowing their choices than finding books to read.

Reason Number 3: Reading aloud builds a sense of community. The community of readers built through reading aloud supports the kinds of interactions and responses we want students to construct in transaction with the literature we share with them. We share our favorite books, chapter books, informational texts, authors, and illustrators with our students and invite them to discover favorites on their own. As teachers, we demonstrate what competent and lifelong readers do, encouraging students to share their responses and ideas with us and each other. In essence, reading aloud and the community of readers we develop creates a "space" for discussions to occur, for relationships to become established, for diverse interpretations to be shared, and for students to learn to respond emotionally to the literature we share.

Stanley Fish (1980) talks about building "interpretive communities" of readers, and about how these communities support the types of readers and the interpretations made by readers in our classrooms. Through the shared experience of reading aloud, students learn to listen to each other's ideas and opinions about particular pieces of literature. They learn to respect the diverse interpretations made possible by quality pieces of literature. Not only does reading aloud support individual readers, it also develops relationships between teachers and students, and among students themselves. These relationships in turn support individual readers and help them learn to read and interpret pieces of literature.

Reason Number 4: *Reading aloud provides opportunities for extended discussions.* By sharing their ideas, students learn that there is more than one interpretation for works in literature and that through discussion, we learn more about a book than we are able to on our own. Vygotsky (1962) suggested that what individuals can do with the help of others is greater than what they can do alone. This is the foundation for the learning in a community of readers.

Reason Number 5: *Reading aloud with older readers is pleasurable.* Learning does not have to be boring and confusing. Reading aloud is a pleasurable experience where students can laugh at stories, share the challenges of their favorite characters, and become involved in the twists and turns of a good plot. Teachers can demonstrate their own joys and love of reading and particular pieces of literature and can create a pleasant experience for the readers in their classrooms.

Reason Number 6: *Reading aloud connects readers with content area subjects.* Reading aloud with older readers provides the knowledge base needed to understand content area subject matter. It is also an easy way to introduce new concepts to students. Picture books have been published that cover a vast array of topics from aardvarks to zebras. Books about geology, family relationships, the American Revolution, Paraguay, dolphins, and many other topics are available in informational and fictional structures. Reading aloud provides students with easy access to new topics and gives them an opportunity to discuss their ideas and questions as they discover new information and concepts. Picture books are well suited to content area discussions. These books increase students' interest in new concepts and encourage them to delve into topics on their own.

Reason Number 7: Reading aloud demonstrates response strategies. Reading aloud with older readers allows teachers to demonstrate the types of responses to literature we want them to construct and share. Students need to learn how to respond to literature in new ways and from new perspectives. Simply finding the main idea may help them on a standardized test, but won't help them become part of a community of readers. As classroom teachers, we want readers to be able to examine a piece of literature from multiple perspectives and discuss their ideas with other classmates. We want students to become literature explorers, reading to understand the story as well as how it was constructed.

Reason Number 8: Reading aloud increases readers' interest in independent reading. Many of our students have become avid independent readers because of the invitations the classroom read alouds offer. In fact, many of the books we used in our first years as teachers had been read to us in our teacher education classes. We read what we are exposed to and what is available to us. Reading aloud is the key to the world of literature; it is our duty to open the door for our students.

Reason Number 9: Reading aloud provides access to books that readers may not be able to experience on their own. Every book is available to every student simply by altering the approach to reading it. When students can't read a book on their own, we can read it to them. Reading aloud provides an important scaffold as young readers increase their independent reading abilities. It allows them to focus on the meanings being constructed rather than on their ability to decode text. Students eventually develop knowledge concerning how books work, the type of "book language" contained in stories, directionality, and other concepts of print and story elements and structures. These concepts and abilities play an important role as readers develop into independent, successful readers.

Reason Number 10: Reading aloud provides demonstrations of oral reading and fluency. Classroom teachers are students' primary guides into the world of literature. Not that we all have to sound like James Earl Jones when we read, but we are demonstrating the ways that reading a book aloud sounds. As skilled readers, we read aloud with fluency and confidence, two skills we want our students to develop. We use voices to bring the stories to life. We demonstrate the way stories are constructed and the way language in books differs from that in oral speech.

Reason Number 11: Reading aloud helps readers understand the connection between reading in school and reading in life. Stories are an important part of our lives both in and out of school. We tell others our own stories so that they may get to know us. Authors share stories so we may get to know them. They invite students to make connections between the story worlds they create and the world in which we live. The ability to connect one's reading and one's life is an important skill readers use to make sense of their literary experiences.

Reason Number 12: Reading aloud provides demonstrations of quality writing. As the old saying goes, "Be careful what you read, for that is how you will write." The books we read aloud provide powerful models for the types of writing students will do. They increase students' vocabulary, which in turn helps them to become better writers. Using authors as mentors, students learn a variety of writing styles and elements of craft.

Reason Number 13: Reading aloud supports readers' development. Besides being an enjoyable experience that builds community, helps readers respond to literature, exposes readers to new titles and authors, invites readers into the world of literature, and creates lifelong readers, reading aloud helps readers become better readers. Reading aloud with older readers provides an opportunity to hear diverse interpretations, share ideas with other students, and expand their own interpretive skills. As we read aloud, we are able to demonstrate the things that competent readers do. These demonstrations are powerful lessons for developing readers.

There is no substitute for reading aloud. No other experience or instructional strategy can capture the mood and enjoyment of a piece of literature. Reading aloud is about more than increasing standardized test scores and developing more capable decoders. It's about teaching children *why* to read, not just *how* to read. It's about inviting them into the world of literature and exposing them to the joys of reading and the fantastic story worlds available in books. It's about teaching them what pleasures await them between the covers of a good book. Shirley Brice Heath (1994) explains that in order to have literate people emerge from our classrooms, we have to provide examples of "joyfully literate adults" for students to emulate. This may be one of the most important roles the teacher plays in their classroom—"joyful promoter of literature and reading."

Finding time in an already overcrowded school day can certainly be a challenge. Those things that we value tend to stay in our schedules, and those things that don't matter as much seem to fade into the background of the curriculum. This chapter makes the case for reading aloud to be one of those things that we value and that will continue to occur every day. With mounting pressure from political groups, standards legislation, and mandated instructional practices, aspects of the curriculum that cannot be defended may disappear. We hope that reading aloud will not suffer such a fate.

Human beings come to know the world through the stories we hear and tell. Since the time of Homer's *Odyssey*, people have used stories to explain nature and the events in the world, to share adventures, and to help young people understand the possible challenges that await them as they grow up. Reading aloud provides the space and opportunity for storytelling to occur every day in our classrooms. For these reasons, we have chosen to read aloud with older readers for many years in our classes, from kindergarten through college.

3
Making Meaning with Text and Illustrations

*There is no substitute for real books. They are rarely boring or sani-
tized or squeezed into a "reading system" that children can smell a
mile off. So logic says if we want real readers we must give them real
books; give our young people good literature, good art, and surpris-
ingly, these young people may do the rest.*

TOMIE DePAOLA
Children's Literature in the Reading Program

Picture books are a unique format, primarily associated with the world of children's and young adult's literature. A quick trip to the nearest bookstore or public library will attest to the multitudes of new picture books available in a wide variety of gen-res, topics, and styles. Approximately three thousand new picture books were published last year alone. That means nearly thirty-five thousand new picture books have been published since 1990!

The picture book format contains many genres, including mysteries, fantasies, traditional stories, poetry anthologies, and biographies.

As the opening quote suggests, the picture books in this text are considered exam-ples of authentic literature—literature that has been written for the trade market, not books written to teach reading skills or contained in a reading instructional series "that children can smell a mile off." Issues of authenticity and relevance to the lives of our students are important considerations as we choose books for our classroom libraries and for our students to read. We select books that tell wondrous stories, take readers on great adventures, present readers with unique perspectives on the world, and help readers vicariously experience places and events they would not in reality. We do not choose books because they contain numerous examples of short *a* vowels or because they teach children sequencing skills.

Picture books are generally a child's first encounter with literature. They provided the entrance through which many of us stepped as we began our lives as readers. It is our job to ensure that children's experiences with literature are powerful ones.

Readers read to enjoy stories, to learn about the world, to inform themselves, to escape, and for numerous other reasons. They don't choose to read literature to get better at reading. It is the story, the beautiful language, and the unique characters that attract us, bring us back to favorite titles, and entice us to explore new ones. If we give readers good literature, there comes a time when we, as teachers, can step out of the way and let the story and illustrations speak for themselves.

Throughout the book, we use the word *text* to describe the written words, the language of the story, and the word *illustrations* to refer to the artwork contained in the picture book. We also refer to other design features such as the fonts, layout, and graphic design elements contained therein. All of these are carefully selected by the author, publisher, and illustrator to narrate the story, to provide the reader with cues to make sense of the story, and to help the reader develop a more sophisticated understanding of the characters, settings, plots, and themes presented.

Picture books, as we refer to them here, are different from illustrated storybooks, where the illustrations are simply an add-on to the story, sometimes created years after the story was written. The picture books we are referring to utilize both illustrations and text. Although these appear as separate entities, they work in concert to narrate the story. Take away either one, and there will be a loss of meaning. Meaning is represented in language and images, inviting the reader to attend to both in order to make sense of the story. Readers are required to navigate the text, illustrations, and design elements in order to construct their understandings. Before discussing the relationship between illustrations and text and how these two systems of meaning narrate the story, we briefly discuss the theoretical framework of the reading process and the construction of meaning in transacting with texts and illustrations. We hope this brief discussion will provide the reader with a theoretical basis for the examples and discussions to follow.

Reader Response Theories

This book operates from a reader response perspective. In other words, it assumes that reader, text, and context are equally important elements in the construction of meaning that occurs during the reading event. Our ideas were greatly influenced by literary theorists and literacy educators who align themselves with this perspective, including Louise Rosenblatt, Stanley Fish, Wolfgang Iser, Patrick Dias, Judith Langer, Kathleen McKormick, Perry Nodelman, and Richard Beach. Although these theorists have different slants on reader response theory, certain central assumptions are common to all. These central assumptions form the foundation for our theoretical framework.

First, reading is the active process of constructing meaning in transaction with the text and illustrations contained in a picture book. Readers bring their knowledge of the world and their knowledge of language, in particular written language, to the reading event in order to make sense of a piece of literature. Like Rosenblatt, we believe that meaning is constructed in the transaction between a particular reader and a particular text in a unique time, place, and sociocultural context.

Second, readers do not exist, or read, in a vacuum. The meanings readers construct are always supported and limited by the context in which they are reading. The immediate and primary context under consideration in this book is the upper elementary and middle school classroom. This is an important consideration. Reading in school is different from reading everyplace else. The environment of the classroom and the community of readers created therein have a tremendous impact on how readers construct their roles as reader and the interpretations they construct during the read aloud experience. The community of readers that develops in a classroom also has a powerful effect on the meanings shared and negotiated by individual readers. The act of reading is a social event, one that always takes place in a social context, even if one is reading alone. Meaning, language, and understandings are created in a social milieu and are constantly being revised due to new experiences.

Third, the text, design elements, and illustrations provided in the picture book being read both limit and support the possible meanings being constructed by the reader. Not only do the reader's background, social experiences, and culture play a role in the meanings constructed, so does the story being read. Many reader response theorists neglect or downplay the role of the text and illustrations in the reading event. Like Rosenblatt, we see this as a mistake. We don't want the books we read aloud to "leave the building" during our discussions. Meanings are constructed in transaction *with* a text. Both readers *and* texts are important aspects of the reading event. When the readers' comments no longer have any relation to the text shared, the text becomes a Rorschach inkblot, and readers begin to free associate. The transaction depends upon the reader; however, it does not ignore the role of the text and illustrations.

Fourth, a text by itself carries no meaning. On the pages of a picture book are simply ink marks and colors. Meaning is created through the interaction of these various symbols as the reader begins reading. The text and the illustrations only have meaning during their transaction with a reader, as the reader brings the story to life during the reading event. Readers must be active participants in the reading process, constructing meaning and connecting references made in the text with the world they live in. Rosenblatt suggests that texts are sources of intellectual and emotional experience.

In order for these experiences to be realized or evoked, a reader must be present. We cannot forget, however, that readers are always reading in a sociocultural, historical, and political context.

Fifth, because readers don't live in a vacuum, Stanley Fish's (1980) conception of an interpretive community is an important consideration in thinking about reading and readers. Although we are reluctant to take the meanings constructed completely out of the readers' heads, we recognize the tremendous impact the context and the community of readers plays on an individual's interpretations of illustrations and texts. Because we believe context plays such an important role, we address the development of communities of readers in Chapter 5. For now, let's say that the context of the reading event is as important as what the reader and the text bring to the reading transaction. Figure 3–1 represents our understandings of the reading event. All three indices of this triangle—readers, texts and illustrations, and the context of the reading event—play a key role in the meanings constructed, shared, and negotiated during the read aloud experience. Each element is a part of the reading event; they cannot be separated.

Sixth, readers respond to texts and illustrations for a range of reasons, and these reasons determine how we read a piece of literature and what we take away from the event. Readers respond differently to different types of texts. For our purposes here, we focus on readers' transactions with picture books, but address chapter books, poetry, and informational texts as well. Why we read a book is as important a consideration as what we read and what background knowledge we bring to the reading event. We read the morning newspaper differently than the way we read an astrophysics textbook. Different purposes, different readings.

Finally, reader response theory calls into question the assumption of a single correct or main idea that resides *within* a text. From a reader response perspective, multiple interpretations can be constructed from a single text, and it is in the negotiation of meaning in the social context of the classroom that possible interpretations

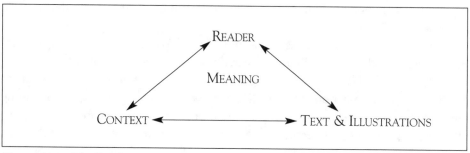

Figure 3–1. The Reading Process

are sanctioned or rejected. This assumption questions the need for a literary canon or the use of Cliff Notes for students to learn the "true" meaning of a piece of literature. Meanings are negotiated in the community of readers. Viable interpretations are warranted or rejected depending on the interactions of the community members. There is no single truth waiting out there to be discovered. We create our own understandings as we interact with other readers.

In summary, reader response theories place the reader in a prominent position during the reading event, without negating the role of the text and the context of the reading. Multiple interpretations of texts are supported through classroom discussions, where readers actively create, share, and negotiate meaning in transaction with a particular text and series of illustrations.

Text, Illustrations, and Something In-Between

Now, let's focus on what happens when readers transact with picture books. It's important to mention that unless the author and illustrator are one and the same person, they often do not collaborate during the creation of the book. Generally speaking, the author submits a written manuscript to a publishing house, which then assigns the work to a particular illustrator. The illustrator conducts extensive research on the setting of the story and the characters described in the manuscript. The illustrator interprets the author's text and creates illustrations to accompany it. Possibly the first time the author sees the illustrations is when the gallies have been completed. Although this may sound unusual, most authors we know and have talked to are quite pleased with the work of the illustrator.

For the illustrator, as well as the reader, the construction of the illustrations and the meanings associated with the written text is an interpretive process. The illustrator adds images to the written text created by the author. This is important to understand. Just as the reader brings her understandings of the world and written language to bear on the text, so does the illustrator. Choosing a particular medium and illustration technique, the illustrator represents his interpretations of the written text. The images created are then included, along with the text and the graphic elements (fonts, titles, borders, layout), for the reader to interpret during their reading of the picture book.

Readers of picture books transact with the illustrations, the written text, and the relationship between the two in order to make meaning. It is important to understand the contributions made by both illustrations and text, but it is even more important, we believe, to understand how they interact with each other to construct a coherent whole.

To begin with, text and illustrations are different, obviously. They present ideas and information in different ways. For instance, text is linear. You follow the progression of words in the English language from left to right and down the page. Readers generally begin reading literature on the first page and proceed through the text to the end of the story. Nonfiction and informational texts may be read differently, of course.

Illustrations are not linear. We see them instantaneously. We may scan different parts of an illustration at different times, but the illustrations are presented all at once. Like a painting or a photograph, we see the complete image presented as a whole. In picture books, the fact that illustrations are presented in a series simply adds to the complexity of the picture book format. Each illustration comes before and after some other illustration (except the front and back covers, of course). The meanings of individual illustrations, therefore, depend on their relationships to the other illustrations in the sequence of the story.

Picture book formats can range from illustrated storybooks, where the text is responsible for narrating the story and the illustrations merely serve as an add-on decoration, to wordless picture books, where the story is narrated completely through the illustrations. In between these two ends of the continuum are the types of picture books we are referring to here. These picture books, as mentioned previously, utilize both illustrations and text to narrate the story; however, the relationships within this category of picture books can vary as well, and these relationships refer to that "in-between" mentioned in the title of this section.

Although the terminology used to describe the relationships between text and illustrations varies from theorist to theorist and educator to educator, generally they refer to three types of relationships or interplay: symmetrical, complementary, and contradictory. In the first type, the text and the illustrations may echo each other; that is, the meanings represented are symmetrical in nature, with practically the same information offered in both texts and illustrations. Of course, it can never be exactly the same information, but the text and illustrations closely parallel each other. For example, there is a picture of a ball in the grass and the text says, "The ball is in the grass." Young readers often use the illustrations in this type of picture book to decode the written text. It is a very basic relationship where little new information is offered in the interplay between text and illustrations.

In the second type of relationship, the text and illustrations complement each other, enhancing what is represented in each alone. Using our example from above, the ball may be sitting in the grass, but now we see a boy running toward the ball and a baseball game going on in the background of the illustration. The ball that is sitting in the grass is no longer just sitting there. The illustration offers more to the story than the text itself. This relationship is considered complementary or enhancing. The text is enhanced by the illustrations. Most picture books we read aloud in our classrooms and will share with you throughout this book fall within this category.

The third type of relationship has been called contradictory or counterpoint. In this type of relationship, the story offered in the text somehow deviates from what is offered in the illustrations. The ball is no longer simply sitting in the grass, it has sprung legs and is sitting cross-legged in a park. Perry Nodelman (2003) describes the tension created between text and illustration as an "ironic" relationship where what is offered in the text is somehow contradicted by the illustrations. Many new picture books that draw upon postmodern techniques often use this relationship to challenge the reader and to disrupt the linear qualities of the traditional picture book. What is important to remember about these three types of relationships is that we can no longer simply focus on the text and the illustrations separately. Discussing the artistic techniques and qualities of a picture book is important, but more important is how the use of particular media influences the book as a whole and interacts with the written text. As teachers of literature, we need to help readers interrogate the relationship between the text and the illustrations to come to more sophisticated understandings of what is offered in the picture books we share.

Why Is This Important?

Why is all of this discussion about the art in picture books and the relationship between illustrations and text important? We believe there is much more to the picture books being shared with students that goes unnoticed because teachers do not have the experience, or the literary and artistic vocabulary, to help children investigate the various elements included in picture books. In order for teachers, teacher-docents, to support readers' explorations of picture books, we need to know as much as possible about the design elements, writing craft, illustration techniques, and dynamics of the text-illustration relationship.

As Lawrence Sipe (1998) has written, there is more to a picture book than the text plus the illustrations. He has called the interplay between text and illustrations a "synergistic" one, suggesting that the whole is greater than the sum of its constituent parts. We agree. This just may be the component most overlooked by teachers when sharing picture books during the read aloud experience.

In a picture book there are two systems of meaning being used to narrate the story: the visual and the verbal. Like Rosenblatt's transactional theory of reading, we don't see these two elements as separate entities, but as elements that make up the literary work as a whole. The text affects the illustrations and the illustrations affect the text.

Illustrations provide information instantaneously, while text is temporal, sharing its information over time. These two types of representations transact in this hybrid format of literature known as the picture book to create a unique and powerful literary experience. As readers go back and forth between illustrations and text, they are forced to *transmediate* or transfer understandings between the two systems of meaning presented. This forces readers to construct a deeper sense of the story than if only one system was used in telling the story.

In contemporary society, children are bombarded with visual imagery. As teachers, we need to help them make sense of these experiences. The picture book provides an excellent opportunity to do just that. The process of transacting with picture books is a recursive one, where readers go back and forth between illustrations and text and forward and backward throughout the book, revisiting illustrations to make sense of the story as they navigate the book's complexities. Each in its own way helps the reader attend to important information in the story. Illustrations don't simply retell what is offered in the text. Rather, they enhance or contradict the text and bring unique perspectives to the story being told. It is through the dynamic interplay between text and illustration that the story emerges.

4

Art Elements and Techniques in Picture Books

The world of children's book illustrations, particularly picture books, continues to grow and evolve, adapting new forms and expanding levels of creativity. This specialized artistic field is inviting, rewarding, and some might say, on the "cutting edge." Children's book illustrators are designing wonderfully exciting and appealing art in children's books.

JULIE CUMMINS
Children's Book Illustration and Design

When reading a picture book aloud, most listeners' eyes will immediately be drawn to the illustrations. As the story is read, there will be interpretations of both the text and of the art as discussed in Chapter 3. In order to take that interpretation to a deeper level, it is important to understand the decisions that illustrators make in order to convey meaning through their art.

Soon after Cyndi was elected to serve on the 2002 Caldecott Award committee, she realized that it was imperative to broaden and strengthen her knowledge of art elements, techniques, and styles. She had to look beyond the immediacy of the picture on the page to the possible meaning that the illustrator is trying to convey through the use of line, color, space, texture, and perspective. Caldecott committee members also have to be able to speak knowledgably about the techniques the illustrator employs and what "distinguishes" the illustrations in a certain picture book. Teachers must be able to do the same. We return to the idea of teacher as docent, able to guide students through a book while assisting them in being able to interpret illustrations along with text. Becoming aware of the elements of art as well as the media used in creating illustrations allows teachers to support students as they "read" the illustrations of a picture book.

Elements of Art

The elements of art are the visual tools that illustrators use to create art. Some of these elements include line, color, shape, texture, and perspective. When all of these elements come together, it creates the composition of the illustration and page. In turn, it assists readers in generating meaning from the story. Following is a discussion of some of these art elements and examples of books that incorporate them effectively.

Line

An important element of art is line. Line can be created by the stroke of a pen, pencil, brush, chalk, fingers, or other medium. Artists use different types of lines to create meaning. Some of these include:

- *Horizontal* Horizontal lines suggest peace or relaxation.
- *Vertical* Vertical lines indicate stability.
- *Diagonal* Diagonal lines suggest motion and movement. Plunging diagonal lines can convey falling, a loss of control, or speed.
- *Circular* Circular lines suggest serenity, contentment, or safety.
- *Chaotic* Chaotic or unorganized lines can suggest disorder, chaos, and frenetic feelings.
- *Thin* Thin lines may have an elegant quality or suggest fragility.
- *Thick* Thick or bold lines can suggest strength or provide emphasis.

In Andrea Davis Pinkney's story *Duke Ellington: The Piano Prince and His Orchestra*, artist Brian Pinkney illustrates the entertaining text with his distinctive scratchboard illustrations. Scratchboard is created by painting black ink on the smooth white surface of a drawing board or scratchboard. When the ink is dry, a sharp instrument produces the picture, and myriad of lines. Color can then be added, as Pinkney did in the story about Duke Ellington. Bright, swirling colors and lines provide a sense of movement and rhythm that are a perfect complement to the story of this jazz giant. See Figure 4–1 for other books that use line effectively.

Color

Color is critical in creating the mood or tone of the story. Color can be limited to a defined range such as black and white and various shades of gray or it may cover a

BAYLOR, BYRD. 1986. *I'm in Charge of Celebrations*. Ill. Peter Parnall. New York: Aladdin.

GERSTEIN, MORDICAI. 1999. *The Absolutely Awful Alphabet*. San Diego, CA: Harcourt Brace.

JONELL, LYNNE. 1999. *It's My Birthday Too!* Ill. Petra Mathers. New York: Putnam.

SCHAEFER, CAROL LEXA. 1996. *The Squiggle*. New York: Crown.

SHULEVITZ, URI. 1969. *Rain Rain Rivers*. New York: Farrar, Straus & Giroux.

VAN ALLSBURG, CHRIS. 1982. *Ben's Dream*. Boston: Houghton Mifflin.

YENAWINE, PHILIP. 1991. *Lines*. New York: Delacorte.

Figure 4–1. Use of Lines in Illustrations

full spectrum. Artists use color schemes as a way of organizing color. Some of these schemes may be:

- *Complementary colors* Colors that are opposite each other on the color wheel. For example, red is the complement of green and blue is the complement or orange. When two pure complementary colors are placed next to each other they create a feeling of excitement.
- *Analogous colors* Colors next to each other on the color wheel that have a common hue such as yellow-green, green, and blue-green.
- *Tertiary colors* Colors produced by mixing two secondary colors, such as green and purple. Brown is a tertiary color.

There are also *warm colors,* which are yellow, orange, and red on the color wheel, and *cool colors,* which are green, purple, and blue on the color wheel. Warm colors create a warm, sunny feeling. Cool colors produce a cold, icy feeling. When they are used together, cool colors seem to move away from the reader while warm colors move toward the reader. There are various symbolic meanings of color. A few of them are:

- *Red* is an attention-getting color that can signify excitement and happiness or danger and courage.

- *Yellow* is the color of sunshine, which makes it a happy color. Some street signs use yellow to urge caution to drivers.
- *Blue* is a restful color. It can convey calmness and tranquility. It can also indicate coldness and sometimes sadness.
- *Green* is a color we associate with nature. It is sometimes viewed as a restful color.
- *Orange* is often associated with the fall season. It is a warm and cheerful color.
- *Purple* is a mixture of blue and red and is linked with royalty. It can be viewed as a color that suggests power and importance.

Author/illustrator Molly Bang is known for her successful use of art elements, especially color. In *When Sophie Gets Angry—Really, Really Angry*, Bang depicts Sophie's changing moods through the use of intense orange and red hues to show her anger while soothing blues and greens envelope her as she "cools" down. In contrast, in Audrey Wood's *The Napping House*, artist Don Wood uses cool blues and greens to illustrate this cumulative tale of animals engaged in slumber. See Figure 4–2 for more examples of the use of color.

Space

Space can be effectively used to produce a feeling of isolation. It can also depict the fine line between reality and fantasy. Illustrator Molly Bang, in her wordless book *The Grey Lady and the Strawberry Snatcher*, and David Macauley's Caldecott winner *Black and White* use negative space to make the characters or objects appear to be fading into the background or literally hiding. In the classic story *Crow Boy* by Taro Yashima, young

---

CARLE, ERIC. 1998. *Hello, Red Fox*. New York: Simon & Schuster.

CRONIN, DOREEN. 2000. *Click, Clack, Moo: Cows That Type*. Ill. Betsy Lewin. New York: Simon & Schuster.

HOBAN, TANA. 1995. *Colors Everywhere*. New York: Greenwillow.

MCCLOSKEY, ROBERT. 1969. *Make Way for Ducklings*. New York: Viking.

SAY, ALLEN. 1993. *Grandfather's Journey*. Boston: Houghton Mifflin.

YOUNG, ED. 1992. *Seven Blind Mice*. New York: Scholastic.

Figure 4–2. Use of Color in Illustrations

AARDEMA, VERNA. 1975. *Why Mosquitoes Buzz in People's Ears: A West African Tale*. Ill. Leo & Diane Dillon. New York: Scholastic.

CRONIN, DOREEN. 2000. *Click, Clack, Moo: Cows That Type*. Ill. Betsy Lewin. New York: Simon & Schuster.

GEORGE, JEAN CRAIGHEAD. 2000. *How to Talk to Your Cat*. Ill. Paul Meisel. New York: HarperCollins.

WIESNER, DAVID. 1999. *Sector 7*. New York: Clarion.

Figure 4–3. Use of Space in Illustrations

Chibi is ostracized by his classmates and is shown walking far behind the other children as they enter school or sitting at a desk that is removed physically from the other children. Figure 4–3 lists other books that demonstrate the use of space in illustrations.

Texture

The texture found in illustrations provides the illusion that something feels hard or soft, smooth or rough. Often texture is created through collage and invites readers to "feel" the pages. Lois Ehlert's books *Snowballs* and *Feathers for Lunch* use everyday objects and materials that create a layered effect. Denise Fleming produces her own paper to illustrate *Lunch* and *Pumpkin Eye*. Readers will want to touch the pages of these books in an attempt to discover the feel of the illustrations and the texture they produce. Figure 4–4 gives other examples of books that use texture.

BAKER, JEANNE. 2000. *The Hidden Forest*. New York: Greenwillow.

CARLE, ERIC. 1999. *The Very Clumsy Click Beetle*. New York: Philomel.

LIONNI, LEO. 1991. *Matthew's Dream*. New York: Knopf.

REID, BARBARA. 1991. *The Party*. New York: Scholastic.

WISNIEWSKI, DAVID. 1996. *Golem*. Boston: Houghton Mifflin.

Figure 4–4. Use of Texture in Illustrations

Point of View or Perspective

One of the most interesting elements that artists use is perspective. An illustrator uses perspective to provide another point of view or to focus on the action in a story. The perspective is the place or angle from which the reader is viewing the picture. Some of the perspectives that can be found in pictures book are:

- *Bird's-eye view* This occurs when it appears the reader has the sense of looking down on a scene in the book.
- *Worm's-eye view* When readers are looking up at a scene they have a worm's-eye view.
- *Foreground* Artists use the bottom third of an illustration as the foreground. Items or characters are larger in this portion of the picture because they appear closer.
- *Middle ground* The middle third of the illustration is considered the middle ground. Readers' eyes are often drawn to the middle of the page in an illustration and then follow it either down or up. Elements in this portion of an illustration are middle size in comparison to those in the foreground and background.
- *Background* Items or characters in the top third of the illustration will appear to be the smallest in size because they are farther away.

Jane Yolen's *Owl Moon*, illustrated by John Schoenherr, allows readers a bird's-eye view of the child and parent as they go "owling" on a crisp winter's night. The view shifts again when a close-up of an owl is shown within the climax of the story. The *Two Bad Ants* in Chris Van Allsburg's book have a unique perspective of the world with all that they encounter on their excursion into the kitchen. And Don Wood moves the point of view upward as each sleeping figure in *The Napping House* is added until readers are looking directly down as the bed collapses. Figure 4–5 lists other books that use different points of view.

BANYAI, ISTVAN. 1995. *Zoom*. New York: Viking.

JENKINS, STEVE. 1995. *Looking Down*. Boston: Houghton Mifflin.

MACAULAY, DAVID. 1997. *Rome Antics*. Boston: Houghton Mifflin.

VAN ALLSBURG, CHRIS. 1981. *Jumanji*. Boston: Houghton Mifflin.

WICK, WALTER. 1998. *Walter Wick's Optical Tricks*. New York: Scholastic.

Figure 4–5. Use of Point of View in Illustrations

EHLERT, LOIS. 1995. *Snowballs*. San Diego, CA: Harcourt Brace.

FLEISCHMAN, PAUL. 2000. *Big Talk: Poems for Four Voices*. Ill. Beppe Giacobbe. Cambridge, MA: Candlewick.

GIBBONS, GAIL. 2000. *Rabbits, Rabbits, and More Rabbits!* New York: Holiday House.

GRAY, KES. 2000. *Eat Your Peas*. Ill. Nick Sharratt. New York: Dorling Kindersley.

HENKES, KEVIN. 2000. *Wemberly Worried*. New York: Greenwillow.

RASCHKA, CHRIS. 2000. *Ring! Yo?* New York: Dorling Kindersley.

STEVENS, JANET, AND SUSAN STEVENS CRUMMEL. 1999. *Cook-a-Doodle-Doo*. San Diego, CA: Harcourt Brace.

Figure 4–6. Use of Composition in Illustrations

Composition

Composition is the arrangement of color, line, shape, and texture. It is how the artist has "composed" the picture, and it affects the meaning that the picture generates for readers. Composition is how all of the art elements come together to create an interesting and sometimes memorable illustration. At times, an illustrator such as Jan Brett in *The Mitten* will use borders to assist in the composition of each page. Maurice Sendak's *Where the Wild Things Are* incorporates cross-hatching of lines throughout the book, the minimizing and maximizing of space, until the Wild Things are engaged in their wild rumpus, and a warm palette suggests a dreamlike state. Kevin Henkes' picture books, such as *Lilly's Purple Plastic Purse*, effectively use space, color, spot drawings, and borders to convey Lilly's varying emotions. Recognizing how the elements are utilized in the illustrations provides opportunities for discussion as well as response. See Figure 4–6 for other books that use composition effectively.

Bang's *Picture This: How Pictures Work* presents a superb explanation of how the art elements work to convey meaning by using the story of Little Red Riding Hood. This informative book will assist teachers in understanding how art elements work together to create illustrations and how important line, color, space, texture, and composition are in conveying meaning.

Techniques Used in Creating Illustrations

Many publishers have recently begun indicating the type of media used in creating a book's illustrations. This information can usually be located on the back of the title page. In addition, there are a few illustrators who provide an in-depth explanation of the creation of the art for the picture book, which readers enjoy learning about and which, in turn, influences them in their own artwork.

Generally, when a publisher accepts an author's manuscript, an editor is then assigned to work with that individual. The editor finds an artist to illustrate the story. The editor must consider the story's topic as well as the mood or tone of the book. The editor then begins looking through an illustrator's previous work or an artist's portfolio in order to match the story with the art. An illustrator's selection of media certainly is an aspect of this process because the book can look very different depending upon the medium that has been chosen.

Artists use a variety of media to create illustrations. The following descriptions of media and technique, as well as examples of books where illustrators have employed a certain medium, will help raise the level of understanding for teachers and readers.

Watercolor

Watercolor appears to be the most prevalent of the media used by illustrators of picture books. Many illustrators feel it is versatile and can create a variety of looks. Some watercolor illustrations have a transparent and often pastel look to them. This pastel look assists in conveying a softer, more calming effect. Other times, watercolors may appear dark or ominous, to add an emotional level such as fear or loneliness to a story. And watercolors can create a warm and cozy effect through the use of multiple layers of paint. There are several techniques that artists use with watercolors. They may include:

- *Wash* This occurs when the brush is loaded up with plenty of water to assist in smoothing the pigment on the paper. Varying proportions of water can create different values and create a transparent effect.
- *Opaque* The artist touches the tip of the brush with water and then loads it up with lots of pigment. This produces a darker color that can be lightened by adding more water.
- *Layering* The more layers of watercolor paint the artist applies, the darker the painting becomes. Layering also enables the artist to change colors, or to allow many different colors to show through.

Peter Catalanotto is a master of watercolor illustrations. He varies his palette to convey somber or playful tones. Catalanotto's artistry in *An Angel for Solomon Singer* by

---

BURLEIGH, ROBERT. 1999. *Hercules*. Ill. Raul Colón. San Diego, CA:
   Silver Whistle/Harcourt Brace.

SCHNACHNER, JUDITH BYRON. 1998. *Mr. Emerson's Cook*. New York: Dutton.

STANLEY, DIANE. 2000. *Michelangelo*. New York: HarperCollins.

STEWART, SARAH. 1995. *The Gardener*. Ill. David Small. New York: Farrar,
   Straus & Giroux.

WILLIAMS, VERA. 1982. *A Chair for My Mother*. New York: Greenwillow.

Figure 4–7. Watercolors

Cynthia Rylant utilizes darker tones as well as reflection to tell the story of an Indiana man trying to find his "home" in New York City. Other artists who use watercolor include Peter Spier, Uri Shulevitz, Allen Say, and Ted Lewin. See Figure 4–7 for additional books that use watercolor.

Crayon and Colored Pencil

Very few illustrators use these two mediums to create their artwork. Crayon is difficult to work with because it does not blend easily and cannot be layered to produce other colors. In using crayons, the topic of the book may influence the medium such as Lynne Jonell's *It's My Birthday Too!* told from a child's perspective and illustrated

---

BURNINGHAM, JOHN. 1983. *Come Away from the Water Shirley*. New York:
   Crowell. (crayon)

LIONNI, LEO. 1970. *Fish Is Fish*. New York: Pantheon. (crayon)

SEYMOUR, TRES. 1993. *Hunting the White Cow*. Ill. Wendy Anderson
   Halperin. Freemont, CA: Orchard. (pencil)

KAY, VERLA. 1999. *Gold Fever*. Ill. S. D. Schindler. New York: Putnam.
   (colored pencil)

RYAN, PAM MUNOZ. 1999. *Amelia and Eleanor Go for a Ride*. Ill.
   Brian Selznick. New York: Scholastic. (colored pencils and graphite)

Figure 4–8. Crayon and Colored Pencil

by Petra Mathers. Colored pencils are also limited in their appearance even though they are more flexible and are generally used with another medium to enhance a look. Stephen Gammell is best known for using colored pencils for Karen Ackerman's Caldecott Award winner, *Song and Dance Man*, and Cynthia Rylant's *The Relatives Came*. Figure 4–8 lists other works that use crayon or colored pencil.

Pastels

Pastels are drawing sticks that can be chalk based or oil based. Most artists use soft pastels, which are easy to apply and creamy to blend. Pastels can also be intermixed to generate new colors. Illustrators may use smooth or textured paper to give the pastels different visual effects. Pastels may be used with other mediums, such as watercolor and ink, as is done in Judith St. George's Caldecott Award winner, *So You Want to Be President?* illustrated by David Small. The texture of the chalk is easily identifiable throughout the book and creates a layered effect. At times pastels are used because the topic lends itself to this medium. Figure 4–9 lists other works that feature pastels.

Acrylics

Acrylics are often compared to oil paints, but there are some distinct differences. Acrylics are water based and dry very quickly. Also, acrylics often produce an even and somewhat flat look in illustrations as opposed to oils on canvas, which can generate more of a texture. Barbara Cooney's recognizable folk-art style is rendered in acrylics in books such as *Miss Rumphius*, *Eleanor*, and *Basket Moon*. See Figure 4–10 for others.

HENDERSHOT, JUDITH. 1987. *In Coal Country*. Ill. Thomas B. Allen. New York: Knopf.

MARTIN, RAFE. 1985. *Foolish Rabbits's Big Mistake*. Ill. Ed Young. New York: Putnam.

MYERS, WALTER DEAN. 2000. *The Blues of Flats Brown*. Ill. Nina Laden. New York: Holiday House.

WINTER, JEANETTE. 1998. *My Name Is Georgia: A Portrait by Jeanette Winter*. San Diego, CA: Silver Whistle/Harcourt Brace.

Figure 4–9. Pastels

ADLER, DAVID. 2000. *America's Champion Swimmer: Gertrude Ederle*. Ill. Terry Widener. San Diego, CA: Harcourt.

COOPER, FLOYD. 1994. *Coming Home: From the Life of Langston Hughes*. New York: Philomel.

CURLEE, LYNN. 1999. *Rushmore: Monument for the Ages*. New York: Scholastic.

WINTER, JONAH. 2002. *Frida*. Ill. Ana Juan. New York: Scholastic.

Figure 4–10. Acrylic Painting

Oil Paints

Many times oil paintings are done on canvas, which often adds a slight texture to the illustrations if readers look closely. However, oil paintings may also be done on wood, paper, or cardboard. Fewer illustrators use oil paints because they take much longer to dry than other media. Michael Dooling tells a story through his illustrations in *The Memory Coat*, the story of a family arriving at Ellis Island. Dooling uses oil on canvas to display the emotions as well as historical setting of this event. Joe Cepeda uses colorful oil paintings to illustrate stories such as Pam Munoz Ryan's *Mice and Beans*. This humorous story focuses on Rosa Maria's preparations for her granddaughter's birthday party—with a little bit of help from some energetic mice. Cepeda's illustrations are shown from the various perspectives of both human and rodent. Figure 4–11 lists other examples of oil paints in picture book illustrations.

BURLEIGH, ROBERT. 1998. *Home Run*. Ill. Mike Wimmer. San Diego, CA: Silver Whistle/Harcourt Brace.

LOCKER, THOMAS. 2002. *Walking with Henry: Based on the Life and Works of Henry David Thoreau*. Golden, CO: Fulcrum.

PAUL, ANN WHITFORD. 1999. *All by Herself: 14 Girls Who Made a Difference*. Ill. Michael Steirnagle. San Diego, CA: Harcourt Brace.

ROCKWELL, ANNE. 2000. *Only Passing Through: The Story of Sojourner Truth*. Ill. R. Gregory Christie. New York: Knopf.

Figure 4–11. Oil Painting

Collage

Collage is derived from the French term *coller* meaning "to glue." This technique consists of cutting and pasting natural or manufactured materials to a painted or unpainted surface. Artists may also use newspaper, wallpaper, photographs, cloth, string, or other materials that assist in creating texture as well as a three-dimensional effect. *Smoky Night*, written by Eve Bunting and illustrated by David Diaz, received the 1995 Caldecott Medal and provides an excellent example of both acrylic painting and collage. *Smoky Night* tells the story of the Los Angeles riots and the neighborhood it impacts. Diaz used broken glass, cereal, dry-cleaning bags, matches, and other materials for the background, which he then photographed. On top of the collage backgrounds are expressive acrylic paintings that reflect the mood and tone of both violence and compassion. There are numerous illustrators who effectively convey meaning through collage illustrations such as Leo Lionni, Eric Carle, Steve Jenkins, and Simms Taback, and others listed in Figure 4–12.

Woodcuts and Engravings

The Caldecott Award-winning *Snowflake Bentley*, written by Jacqueline Briggs Martin and illustrated by Mary Azarian, is a picture book biography of a Vermont farmer who held a fascination for photographing snowflakes. Azarian has become known for her unique woodcuts in other books such as *When the Moon Is Full: A Lunar Year* by Penny Pollock and *Race of the Birkebeiners* by Lisa Lunge-Larsen. Woodcuts are generated by carving a design in a block of wood. Many illustrators including Azarian then add another medium such as watercolor to complete the overall effect. Figure 4–13 lists other wonderful books that use woodcuts and engraving.

ADOFF, ARNOLD. 2000. *Touch the Poem*. Ill. Lisa Desimini. New York: BlueSky/Scholastic.

CENDRARS, BLAISE. 1982. *Shadow*. Ill. Marcia Brown. New York: Scribner's.

COY, JOHN. 1999. *Strong to the Hoop*. Ill. Leslie Jean-Bart. New York: Lee & Low.

WIESNIEWSKI, DAVID. 1996. *Golem*. New York: Clarion.

Figure 4–12. Collage

BUNTING, EVE. 2001. *Riding the Tiger*. Ill. David Frampton. Boston: Houghton Mifflin.

EMBERLEY, ED. 1987. *Drummer Hoff*. New York: Simon & Schuster.

GEISERT, ARTHUR. 1986. *Pigs from A to Z*. Boston: Houghton Mifflin.

MACLACHLAN, PATRICIA. 1995. *What You Know First*. Ill. Barry Moser. New York: HarperCollins.

Figure 4–13. Woodcuts and Engraving

Digital Computer

One of the newer possibilities of computer use has been in generating graphics to illustrate books. In the early 1990s, the graphics in picture books were flat in appearance. With advancements in computer capabilities, this is beginning to change, as evident when picture book illustrators use software such as Adobe Illustrator or PhotoShop, which can add texture. An excellent example of colorful computer-enhanced illustrations can be found in *alphabet adventure* written by Audrey Wood and illustrated by her son, Bruce. Additional information about this book is located at www.audreywood.com. Figure 4–14 lists other books that make use of computer-enhanced illustrations.

JOYCE, WILLIAM. 1999. *Rolie Polie Olie*. New York: HarperCollins.

MAYER, MERCER. 1999. *Shibumi and the Kitemaker*. New York: Marshall Cavendish.

WILBUR, RICHARD. 1998. *The Disappearing Alphabet*. Ill. David Diaz. San Diego, CA: Harcourt.

WOOD, AUDREY. 1998. *The Christmas Adventure of Space Elf Sam*. Ill. Bruce Wood. New York: Scholastic.

Figure 4–14. Digital Computer

Putting It All Together

The 2002 Caldecott Award-winning book was David Wiesner's *The Three Pigs*. Wiesner was able to effectively incorporate many art elements into his telling of this supposedly traditional story. If readers remove the book jacket they will discover that the spine is the color of bricks, the hardcover front panel is gray, signifying the sticks, and the interior endpages are straw in color. The extensive white space is used to signal that the pigs are leaving one literary world for another while varying angles of the pigs in flight provide a unique perspective of their journey. Curving lines assist the reader's eye in moving from one aspect of the illustration to the next and to the following page. And when readers encounter the garish colors used in the cartoonlike illustrations depicting the world of Mother Goose and fantasy, they know that something dramatic has occurred. No single art element used in *The Three Pigs* is more significant than any other; rather, each assists in the storytelling. Finally, Wiesner has used watercolors to create his illustrations but has also utilized technology to digitally alter some of the pictures, such as the crumpled-up pages of the pigs' story.

As readers become more competent in their visual literacy, they will be able to interpret the illustrations at a deeper level of meaning. As discussed in the previous chapter, the text and illustrations work together in concert to create meaning. Without knowledge of both, the reader cannot realize the book's full potential.

Picture books provide older readers with quality visual images and well-crafted language in an accessible, relatively short, literary format. The variety of topics presented in contemporary picture books and the quality of the illustrations and written language contained therein provide teachers with unique opportunities to help students make sense of their world and investigate important concepts in various content areas and the language arts. Because of their length, picture books can be used to help teachers develop engaging literacy minilessons as well. Contemporary picture books are wonderful resources for connecting read alouds with other parts of the elementary curriculum, for presenting students with examples of quality visual art and images, and for supporting literacy lessons intended for older readers and writers.

5
Setting the Stage

Life in literature-based classrooms is in a constant state of becoming.
Books, children and teachers all count. There is no prescribed plan to
be acted out.

RALPH PETERSON AND MARYANN EEDS
Grand Conversations

Reading aloud with students is an opportunity to set the stage for experiences to come. By reading aloud, we are preparing the foundation for studies and explorations in the language arts and the content areas; such as math, social studies, and science. We are inviting our students to respond to the literature we share with them, to engage with the story in meaningful and sophisticated ways, and to share these responses with the students around them. We are also demonstrating how we hope they will respond to life's experiences.

In other words, students are invited to actively question and reflect on the books we read, just as they are invited to actively question and reflect on the events in their lives. We want them to experience the powerful issues presented in the literature we share with them in order to prepare them to respond to the powerful issues they will encounter in their daily lives. We may be focusing on literature during the read aloud event, but it's really life we are dealing with. It is important to present how we "set the stage" for reading aloud to occur because we know from our own experiences and observations that the classroom community and environment can make or break the quality of the read aloud experience.

Developing a Community of Readers

Classrooms should be places to cultivate and interrogate ideas, and act out human curiosity. It should be a supportive and challenging environment that encourages students to share their ideas, yet challenges them to rethink their assumptions and interpretations.

We want to develop classrooms where democratic principles are not simply talked about and studied, but *enacted* throughout the day. Such principles include the sharing and negotiation of classroom decisions, the empowerment of students, the opportunity for student voices to be heard, and the involvement of both student and teacher in constructing the classroom curriculum. In order for quality discussions around literature to occur, students need to be empowered to share their ideas and openly negotiate the meanings being constructed within the interpretive community. This cannot occur when the teacher stands in front of the room and dominates the discussions like a drill sergeant. Teaching in a democratic classroom is not a one-person show. Students and teachers should be intimately involved in the constructing, sharing, and negotiation of meanings during the read aloud experience. The experiences that occur in connection with the literature we read should reflect the kind of society we want to live in and the future we envision for our students.

There is a fine line between what Peterson and Eeds (1990) call "Grand Conversations" and the literary inquisitions that frequently occur in classrooms. The questions we ask, the expectations we articulate, the community of readers we establish all contribute to how children respond to the literature we share. We don't just jump into dialogue with young readers. We enter through the door of conversation, establishing trust and rapport, working alongside our students to develop more sophisticated interpretations of literature. We share our ideas openly and honestly in hopes that our students will respond likewise. We encourage them to speak their minds and share their impressions, connections, and wonderings about the books we read. We help them make connections among the ideas offered, call attention to the elements and structures of literature as they arise in our discussions, and provide access to the learning that has gone before us through charts and other visual representations.

As effective classroom teachers, we view ourselves as listeners and readers first, and teachers second. This means knowing our craft, the literature that we read, and the students in our charge. We need to extend our knowledge base about the literature we share and the literary theories that inform our practice. As we become more accomplished readers, we learn to become more accomplished teachers of readers.

As university-based teachers, we shudder when we hear our graduate students share with us how much they hate to read. We understand their plight. We sympathize with their position. But we cannot let this declaration go unchallenged. Many of us have been damaged by our educational experiences; however, we wonder how many of you would be comfortable going to a heart surgeon that hates to do surgery, or a fitness trainer that is overweight and hates to work out? It doesn't do any good to love books and not tell anyone. And it doesn't do any good to go around telling everyone if you don't love what you do. We want teachers that teach reading to love what they do.

In addition to places where ideas are supported, our classrooms have to be places of intellectual challenge. Learning thrives in the delicate balance between support and challenge. In other words, we cannot allow ourselves to accept every whimsical, superficial interpretation constructed by our students. Students need to know that they will be asked to provide evidence of their reasoning and that they will be expected to explain how they came up with their ideas and to think about the other possibilities offered during our discussions. We don't want to reduce students' interpretive processes to the search for a single, main idea, nor do we want to adopt an "anything goes," free-association approach to the interpretations that are put forth. It is important to support students' interpretations and transactions with literature, while simultaneously challenging them to analyze these interpretations and provide reasons for their ideas.

For example, when reading *Where the Wild Things Are* with a group of intermediate-grade students, a child offered the following personal connection: "My grandfather has a dog named Max, just like the name of the character in the story." This is a superficial connection, at best. Although we would not dismiss this connection outright, certainly we want to support students' deeper engagement with the story. It seemed, through further discussion, that the book had "left the building." In other words, the response made about the character Max had little or no relationship to anything in the story except his name. In this instance, the book was no longer part of the student's interpretive process or thinking; it had simply become a prompt for his free association of ideas. In other words, we want students to generate more sophisticated, robust interpretations during their transactions with stories.

Most important, readers must come to understand that reading is making meaning with texts. The focus has to remain the construction of meaning, the understanding and appreciation of story. All the skills we teach, and the reading strategies we develop with students, must be in service of making sense of the story. Without meaning there is no reading. When students really understand this concept, we mean *really* understand this concept, many other challenges fall away. For instance, when students are reading for meaning, we don't need to monitor their book choices as closely. Because they are always reading for meaning, they rarely choose inappropriately. We no longer have to color-code or level our library collections in order for them to make appropriate choices—they make them based on the meanings they construct. If meaning is what they expect from texts, then that is what they focus on.

Before we begin to talk about the reading aloud experience in and of itself, we must first describe the rituals and physical characteristics of our read aloud experiences, and then present our criteria for selecting the literature we read aloud. Chapter 6 describes how we actually read aloud—how we hold the book, the voices we use, and the expectations we create for our students.

Rituals and Stage Design

Some of our most memorable moments at the theater have been because of the beautiful set displays that accompanied the plays and musicals we experienced. Extravagant stage decorations helped us leave the real world behind and enter more fully into the fictional world of the play. The same can be true for our classrooms. The stages and rituals that we develop help students enter more fully into our read aloud experiences. As Ralph Peterson (1992), in his remarkable book *Life in a Crowded Place*, has suggested, the rituals we develop with our students help them turn their attention away from the everyday experiences of daily life and enter into the experiences associated with learning in our classrooms.

In our classrooms, we generally begin the day with what we have called "opening ceremonies." We gather on the floor in a place set aside for this purpose and share the important events in our lives. This helps students learn about each other and thus feel more comfortable sharing ideas and interpretations. The brief opening ceremony brings an intellectual and emotional ordering to the events in our room. We use rituals to create certain expectations for our students to follow. The rituals we create allow for smoother transitions throughout the day.

The read aloud experience consists of the entire set of rituals associated with reading aloud a piece of literature. It begins with the gathering together of students and teacher in a particular place in the room. We believe it is important to create a comfortable place where students can put aside all other distractions and focus on the literature being read. Whether this is a corner of the room, part of the classroom library, or a special rug rolled out on the floor, the creation of a space sets the tone for subsequent experiences. Some teachers we know light a special candle, sit in a favorite rocking chair, distribute special pillows, gather under a particular mobile of book covers, or rearrange chairs into a listening circle. The particulars of the ritual are not as important as the fact that you develop one and use it consistently. When this becomes part of the classroom routine, students know exactly what to expect and what is expected of them. Students know when it's time for a read aloud. They know where to go and what to do.

These rituals are symbolic acts that take on meaning in the context of the classroom community. They indicate that readers are taking part in an important event that demands particular expectations and actions. It is through these symbolic acts, through the focusing of attention, that the stage is set for the read aloud experience.

Selecting Literature to Read Aloud

Literature for read aloud is selected in a variety of ways. A teacher may listen to the suggestions made by another classroom teacher or to the newest titles recommended by the school librarian. Teachers may consult professional resources in print journals or on the Internet that advocate the best books to read to children. Or sometimes, they simply spend time in local bookstores of libraries, discovering new books to share with their classes.

Literature is chosen for a variety of reasons. Sometimes teachers may provide a classroom library for students to self-select books for independent reading time. Often these books reflect children's varied interests reflecting pop culture, series titles, and other high-interest books. Other times, teachers read aloud a classic example of children's literature to expose them to the works of art that have come before them. At best, the classroom library is well stocked with both contemporary and classic quality literature.

Teachers send a direct message to their students through the literature they select to read aloud. Why else would there be a mad dash to the library each day to check out the chapter book currently being read aloud? Students believe that if the teacher chooses the book, it must be good.

There are several questions a teacher should ask herself when selecting a book to read aloud.

1. *Have you read the book?* This may appear to be obvious, but we are constantly amazed how often we hear teachers state that they don't read books first before reading them aloud to their students. How can anyone effectively read a story when they are not familiar with the flow of the language, the content of the story, and the various characters' personalities and how they are portrayed? And how can a teacher support student response and discussions related to the book when they are hearing it themselves for the first time? Our role as teachers is not to discover a story with our students but to guide them through the book while navigating the story. Docents know their museums before they take visitors on a tour; teachers need to know the literature they read before taking students on a literary tour.

2. *Did you enjoy the story?* The most successful read alouds are those that you yourself enjoy as a reader. The enjoyment of a particular piece of literature comes through in the passion with which the story is read and contributes to the excitement that is generated for students. You can certainly read a book that you don't find a personal connection with, but in general, they are not as successful as those that you relate to and are your personal favorites.

3. *Does it tell a good story?* Just because a book got published does not mean it is worth reading aloud. There are some incredible stories that have been written and there are some that are less than wonderful. We encourage reading stories that have depth and layers of meaning and that promote discussion and personal response. We want students to make strong connections to the characters and events that take place in the literature we select.

4. *Does it represent high literary and artistic quality?* What is the quality of the writing? Does the language flow? Will it stretch your students' imaginations? Do the illustrations draw the listener in for a closer look? This criterion is similar to the previous one in terms of wanting to bring the best to children, yet it goes beyond the story to look at the book as a whole and at the connectedness between text and illustration. With so many high-quality books being published each and every year, there is simply no reason to read aloud poorly written books with inferior illustrations.

5. *Are the characters well developed and delineated?* This is especially important in realistic fiction stories where the characters drive the story. Their actions and solutions should be believable, and not always ones that we would agree with should we find ourselves in the same situation. Interesting characters that students can connect with often support exciting discussions.

6. *Is the content of the book appropriate for the intended audience?* This is where prereading a story is vital. No teacher wants to be surprised by the death of a character or by gratuitous language. We are certainly not advocating censorship in any form, but there are times when the content of a book may not be appropriate for your students. Even Lois Lowry is appalled when she hears that *The Giver* is being read at the primary level. Sometimes the stories are too complex for the listener or need a certain level of emotional maturity in order for the listener to truly appreciate the content or situations being encountered by the characters. Such decisions are made by classroom teachers who really know the interests, abilities, and experiences of their students.

7. *Will you be successful as a storyteller in reading the book aloud?* There are some stories that work very well as a read aloud. Often they contain language that invites itself to be heard. This also depends on the reader's voice, timing, and intonation patterns, which can effectively convey the mood and tone of the story. Books with heavy dialect sometimes aren't as successful if the storyteller's voice mimics rather than portrays the culture. Also, wordless books or books where the illustrations tell the majority of the story don't work quite as well as a read aloud because the teacher has to interpret the story for the listeners, which in turn takes away their opportunity to create their own meaning and understanding of the story. These books, however, work well with small groups of students when everyone can see the illustrations and is able to contribute to the storytelling.

8. *How does the book enable you to generate and enhance the curriculum?* A teacher recently asked us, "Can't we read a book just for fun?" Of course! There are many books that you will want to share the minute you find them. Go ahead and read them! The majority of your choices for reading aloud, however, especially as you generate curriculum with your students, will be those you can build from throughout the curriculum. As John Dewey (1910, 1938) has suggested, the experiences we have today should build upon the ones we had yesterday and lead to the ones we have tomorrow.

Consider these eight criteria when selecting a book to read aloud to students. Other items to consider include the accuracy of informational books, the portrayal of ethnic and gendered characters, or the authenticity of historical events. We suggest these criteria as a place to start. Teachers should develop their own criteria as they become more and more familiar with children's literature.

6

Performing Literature

"And now," cried Max, "Let the wild rumpus start!"

MAURICE SENDAK
Where the Wild Things Are

When we think about the act of reading aloud with children, we envision it as a performance, a bringing to life of the text and illustrations with a particular reader and audience. In this case, the audience is usually our students and the classroom becomes our stage. Much like a Broadway play, each performance brings new energy and excitement, new expectations, and new opportunities for our read aloud experience. No two performances of a play are ever alike, and no two readings of a book are ever alike. The dynamics between the reader and the audience change even though the script remains the same.

When reading a book on our classroom stage with our students, we need to pay close attention to our performance and the reactions of our audience. We may have to change our pace or alter our tone of voice in response to their reactions. Their smiles and their enthusiasm spur us on to new levels of involvement. Scary books, poetry, nonfiction, and dramatic novels should not be read aloud in the same manner with the same tone of voice. In order to become accomplished performers of the pieces of literature that we share with our students, we need to learn how to adapt our performance to fit the language and mood of the stories we select.

The books we have read aloud time and again—our personal favorites or pieces that contain lyrical language and captivating illustrations—provide some of our best read aloud performances. Standing ovations, so to speak. We read with confidence and passion, enunciating the words and pacing the story to create maximum dramatic effect. But, we don't want our voices or the cadence we use to overpower the story or take away from the wonderful pieces of literature we select. Our oral performance should enhance the story, not detract from it.

We want to create what Don Holdaway (1979) described as the "classroom lap." All our students should feel as if they were sitting comfortably in our laps listening to our specially selected stories. We want each student to develop a one-on-one relationship with the story even if there are thirty children in our classroom. We read loudly and clearly enough so that each student can enter into the story world from wherever they are in our classroom. Hearing stories read aloud is a safe, enjoyable experience that we want to share with each and every one of our students each and every day.

Teachers and librarians ask us many questions about choosing books, reading aloud, and performing literature. We hope these are some of your questions as well, and that our answers will help you create more effective, more dramatic, more enjoyable read aloud experiences.

Question 1: *Do you just read the words on the page, or do you extend the text by "ad-libbing" some of the story as you are reading aloud?* To be honest, we like to ad-lib when we feel it adds to the story and does not detract from the author's language or intentions. Of course, what we think the author's intentions are is quite subjective, but, we feel that performers have the right to put their mark on the piece they are performing. We are not in any way advocating completely altering the author's language or the illustrator's visual images. We respect their work. But be it a play, a piece of music, or a picture book, performers add their own flavor and their own interpretations to the performance. Sometimes we add words or phrases to emphasize a particular point or action. Other times we want to clarify what an author has written and may reread a particular section of text. For the most part, though, we stick to the script, believing that quality pieces of literature will speak for themselves.

The same concern holds true for the voices we use when we are reading. They should sound natural and spontaneous, but may have to be rehearsed in order to sound that way. Some people are better at creating unique voices than others. We know that students, when asked about teachers using different voices during read alouds, have responded overwhelmingly in favor of their use. When students become more interested in the voices you are using than the story being read, however, it may be time to pull back. We have to pay close attention to the effects we are having on our audiences in order to judge whether we are detracting from the story.

Question 2: How do you make the author or illustrator part of the read aloud experience? One way to bring the author and illustrator into our discussions and read alouds is by referring to them as people we know, or feel that we know, when we talk to our students. We say things like, "Look at how William Steig decided to end *Sylvester and the Magic Pebble*," or "I like the way that David Weisner used perspective to portray a sense of flying in his book *Tuesday*." We want to bring the authors and illustrators to life, to portray them as people that live in the same world we live in. We want children to learn that authors create stories, and that they have opinions, fears, and beliefs about the world. We don't want them to think that books just show up on library shelves.

Question #3: How do you deal with the "wigglers" and the "carpet inspectors" when you are reading aloud? We would like to think that we are just so darn good at reading aloud that we basically mesmerize our students into a trance where they could never fathom attending to anything but our voices and the story being read. Unfortunately, we teach in the real world, where children roll around on the floor and pinch each other at times. First of all, we cannot dismiss those children that look like they are not paying attention. We have been fooled time and again by students who don't look like they are listening yet have not missed a beat in the story. We also realize that younger children have different attention spans, so we select our literature accordingly. But most of all, we have tremendous faith in the authors and illustrators that we share the stage with. We know that through our performance of their language and artwork, we can hold more children spellbound than we can bore to pieces. The old adage, "You can't beat good material" holds true. If we have chosen well, if we perform well, if students can connect to the literature we share, we will have fewer wandering minds. Besides, who wants to start every read aloud by telling students to sit up straight and pay attention? We want children who rush to get to the read aloud area to hear another wondrous story. Children should be warmly invited to share literature in our community of readers, not bullied into paying attention.

Question #4: Do you stop during a read aloud and have students predict what will happen next? The best way for us to answer this question is to ask you, "Do you stop when you are reading a good mystery novel to make predictions?" Probably not. However, you are constantly anticipating what will happen and are surprised when things don't turn out the way you expect. We do the same thing. Do we want students to anticipate what will happen? Sure. Do we stop our reading every few pages to ask them to predict what will happen in order to get them to do this? Probably not. We usually spend time before we begin reading a book looking at the cover and end pages in order to get a sense of where we are heading. We want students to activate their prior knowledge and anticipate what may happen in the story; however, interrupting the story too often detracts from students' enjoyment of what is being read. If students naturally predict on their own and offer these ideas in our discussions, that's acceptable, but we don't force that way of responding to texts upon them.

Question #5: *How do you hold the book when you are reading aloud?* We hold the book in one hand so that students can see the illustrations as we read aloud. We do this because it is how author, illustrator, and publisher intended the book to be read. Picture books, as we have described, are created using both text and illustrations to help the reader understand and interpret the story. How can students attend to the illustrations if they can't see them? In keeping with the concept of the classroom lap, if a child was sitting in your lap while you were reading, would you withhold the illustrations until the child had created his own images? Readers attend to the illustrations to make sense of the story. Children attend to the illustrations even more than adult readers. Why withhold this important source of information until the page is finished or the story is completed?

We know some of you want students to create images in their head. We agree with this. One possibility is to use texts that contain no illustrations, for example, chapter books. Students have no choice but to create their own images with these books, since no illustrations are available. Picture books are created using two systems of meaning, text and illustrations. We believe that they should both be made available to the reader simultaneously.

Some picture books tempt us to read the words and then show the illustrations to add to the sense of irony evoked by the relationship between text and illustrations. For example, Rod Clement's *Just Another Ordinary Day* uses straight forward language and outlandish illustrations to create a humorous effect. Another example is Fred Gwynne's series of books containing homonyms, such as *A Little Pigeon Toad* or *A Chocolate Moose for Dinner*. The contradictions and the sense of irony between text and illustration are what make these books so enjoyable. However, if the text is well written, and the illustrations are of high quality, students should be able to enjoy the story in its entirety. When we buy picture books and read them ourselves for the first time, we do not cover the words or hide the illustrations. And guess what? We still enjoy reading them. So will our students. Besides, just because there are illustrations present does not exclude readers from creating images on their own.

Question #6: Do you stop during the reading of the story to allow students to make comments, or do you ask them to wait until the end of the book? This is one of the most frequently asked questions, and one of the most challenging to answer. First, we don't know you or your students. Second, the best answer is, "It depends," and we know you were hoping for a better response, so we will explain what we did.

Frank handled this concern in his own class by allowing students to make comments as he showed the illustrations after reading each page. He would hold the book so everyone could see the illustrations as he was reading aloud, and then he would pass the book in front of the students for their closer inspection of the illustrations. During that time, students would offer ideas, comments, and questions. Then, he would go on to the next page, postponing the bulk of the discussion until after the story had been read.

On the one hand, we want students to be able to offer their ideas and interpretations of the stories we share. On the other hand, we want students to engage with the entire story, taking into consideration that interruptions may affect their engagement. Each of you needs to come to a decision about how you will handle this challenge and be consistent with your expectations so that students understand how they are encouraged to respond during the read aloud experience.

Question #7: Do you ever reread stories you have read before? Absolutely! We revisit favorite stories all the time. We don't want students to think that stories aren't worth revisiting, or that we have exhausted all the possibilities a story presents in one reading. Readers naturally ask to hear stories over and over. Time and again, parents have shared with us stories of a favorite book that they had to read to their child over and over until the book was worn out. Why would we not do the same thing in schools?

Quality literature does not reveal itself completely during the initial reading. As readers of picture books, we have been astounded by the new and varied interpretations our students offer after reading a book for a second and third time. The first time through, students are so interested in what is *going to happen* that they often pay little attention to *how it happens* along the way. Readers often need a second read-through to attend to the language used and carefully study the illustrations to uncover all the treasures that are included in the story. It wasn't until about the tenth reading of *Where the Wild Things Are* that we finally began to realize the complexity of this "simple" children's book. Still today, I am amazed by the new interpretations and new ideas that my students construct during our readings of this classic picture book. Read books again? Of course! We can't afford to miss all the new things that are waiting to be discovered between the covers and during our read aloud discussions.

Question #8: *Where do you stand or sit when you are reading aloud in your classroom?* We have always preferred to sit on a low chair, just above our students heads, in a special place in our classrooms. We want students sitting on the floor so that they can get close to the illustrations and are able to pay attention to the stories we read. We like to be close to our students' eye level, not towering above them, so we choose chairs that allow us this vantage point. We are positioned just above them so each child can see our face and the book we are reading. We would never use a bar stool—too high above the crowds.

We don't allow students to sit at their desks or to draw when we are reading aloud. If we want to teach drawing, we will create time to do that. We want students to engage with our stories and we set those expectations from the first time we read aloud. Sitting in a rocking chair, on a stool, on a couch, or in a special chair is all part of creating rituals around the read aloud. For many of us, simply going over to sit in that special chair signals to our students that it is time for a read aloud and that they are expected to join us there. It is a ritual that is established over time, and students learn what is expected when we signal a read aloud to begin.

Question #9: *What do you do when you are introducing a book to your students before you read it aloud?* Before we ever get to the first page of the story, we spend time with our students discussing the cover, the end pages, the title page, the dedication, the book jacket, the author information, the Library of Congress summary, the publication date, and other information contained in the front matter. There is so much to learn about a book in these pages that to turn to the first page of text and start reading seems foolish.

We want students to activate prior knowledge concerning the story, so we sometimes ask them what they are thinking as they look at the cover and other materials. This helps them anticipate what may occur in the story. Many illustrators and authors put things into these pages to provide clues to the story. They use this space to expand on what happens in the book. Discussions often begin long before we start to read the story aloud. Attending to this information adds to the read aloud performance.

Question #10: *What do you do when you are finished reading a book?* Good question! As a matter of fact, this question is the focus of Part II of *Reading Aloud and Beyond*. So read on!

Effective Read Aloud Performances

As we have stated earlier, research has shown that reading aloud with children helps them become better readers and writers, exposes them to new authors and genres, and provides opportunities to discuss their responses to literature. We finish this first section of the book with a list of some of the common characteristics of quality read aloud experiences.

Effective read alouds

1. have established rituals associated with them, designated times and places for the rituals to occur, established expectations for students, and consistent actions that take place;
2. occur numerous times during the day;
3. include high-quality literature;
4. establish connections with other pieces of literature and aspects of the curriculum;
5. promote discussions before, during, and after reading;
6. support a variety of student responses;
7. are facilitated by knowledgeable teachers;
8. introduce new titles, authors, genres, and illustrators to students;
9. revisit past favorites and classic literature; and
10. take advantage of the teachable moment.

There you have it. Ten characteristics to consider when designing your read aloud experiences. Now that we have discussed preparing for the read aloud experience, selecting literature, and performing the actual read aloud, we turn our attention to what occurs when the read aloud is finished.

7

Response Experiences and Strategies

I have no more right to tell readers how they should respond to what I have written than they had to tell me how to write it.

KATHERINE PATERSON
Gates of Excellence

University students and classroom teachers frequently ask us why we like or don't like particular activities that are designed in response to pieces of children's literature. Some activities are so blatantly horrible that we wonder what the person was thinking when they wrote down these ideas. For example, on the Internet we once saw a lesson plan that had students doing research on groundwater after reading *Tuck Everlasting* by Natalie Babbitt. Another lesson had students reading *Charlotte's Web* by E. B. White before they did their annual unit on spiders. These activities represent superficial connections to the text at best and are indicative of the lower level and shallow experiences often created by commercial reading programs. They don't support quality literary discussions, higher-level thinking, or sophisticated responses to literature.

As we began to explain to students and teachers *why* we didn't like these activities, we were forced to unpack our criteria for quality literary experiences and response strategies associated with reading literature aloud. We realized that we did not like many of the lessons found in commercial programs and on the Internet that were called "activities." Many of them do not meet the criteria we use when evaluating the experiences we provide in our classrooms. For this reason, we have chosen to use the label "experiences" or "response strategies" to refer to the kinds of lessons we would use with our students. We begin this chapter with a brief discussion of the characteristics of the response experiences we would provide and then offer numerous examples and possible response strategies for teachers to use in their classrooms. It is our hope that providing criteria to evaluate the experiences we create in our classrooms will help teachers make better decisions about the experiences they offer.

What Makes a Quality Response Experience?

We believe it is necessary to respect the piece of literature that is being read and discussed. The experiences we provide must have a robust connection to the text, not superficial ones like the examples cited from the Internet. We consider whether the experiences we construct will support students' discussions and engagement with a text. We think about who controls the experience and how much student choice and autonomy is included. Students should have a say in the experiences that occur in their classrooms, and we want to design experiences with this in mind.

We also want the experiences that we provide to be relevant to the lives and to our students' own experiences. In other words, we don't want the things we do with literature to be found only in school settings. We want book discussions to reflect the types of discussions people have outside of schools.

Classroom lessons should build on previous classroom experiences and lead to future experiences. John Dewey (1910, 1938) has articulated the need for the curriculum to be based on the students' experiences and knowledge and to lead to future growth and development. Lessons that have little or no connection to the curriculum and the events in the classroom are not as valuable.

Classroom experiences have a purpose. They are chosen because they help us achieve the goals of reader engagement and students' deeper understandings of the texts they read. They are not created to keep children quiet while we teach a guided reading lesson, nor are they used to teach art or writing skills. The experiences we use in the reading workshop are designed to help readers become more sophisticated in their ability to understand and respond to literature, to provide multiple points of entry, and to allow *all* of our students to understand the lesson and be successful regardless of their prior experiences with literature. The experiences we create should extend students' thinking, support them in adopting multiple viewpoints, include multiple ways of knowing, make connections to other elements of the curriculum, and strengthen their engagement with texts.

Research shows that effective read alouds include high-quality literature; support connections across pieces of literature, genres, and topics; maximize response potential by using multiple ways of grouping students; and include a variety of response strategies and experiences. Reading aloud with students should become a consistent ritual that occurs on a daily basis, and multiple times during the day. Reading aloud with students often involves the rereading of favorite stories, allowing students to delve deeper into the complexities of quality pieces of literature.

Strategies to Assist Students' Thinking

The following learning experiences provide opportunities for students to respond to a piece of literature in order to construct a variety of meanings. They are not comprehension activities, like those found in teachers' basal manuals, but *strategies* that assist students in thinking through their responses to a book.

- *Questions? Questions?* At the conclusion of a picture book or at a natural stopping place in a chapter book, have listeners write down questions they may have about the story and their connections to it. These are not comprehension questions but rather wondering questions that may or may not have a definite answer. As an example, at the end of reading *The Relatives Came* by Cynthia Rylant, which highlights a family who travels to spend time with relatives, one student wrote, "What happens when those kids get older? Do they continue to get together after they have their own kids?"

- *Compare and Contrast* Read alouds shouldn't be selected at random but chosen because they support the curriculum. Within a unit on community, books that feature family reunions such as *The Relatives Came* by Cynthia Rylant and Patricia Polacco's *When Lightning Comes in a Jar* can be compared using a Venn diagram or other tool to show aspects of the story that were the same and different. Comparing and contrasting also works especially well with versions and variants of fairy tales.

- *Conversation Creation* Books such as *Yo! Yes?* or *Ring! Yo?* by Chris Raschka, which provide only half a conversation, allow students to create their own dialogue. *I Am the Dog, I Am the Cat* by Donald Hall shares two perspectives and offers a model for students to do the same with differing viewpoints.

- *Story Quilt* This response strategy works particularly well at the end of a unit of study where literature has been a primary focus or at the conclusion of a chapter book. In each square, students write the following: book title; author and illustrator's names; favorite quote from the book; sketch. Inside the quilt square, students write their connection to the book. Paste each quilt square on a larger square, punch two holes on each side of the larger square, and then tie it together using string or yarn so that it makes a quilt.

- *Stories from the Headlines* Current events are generally a part of intermediate- and middle-level curricula. Many stories in literature relate to events happening in society today or in the past. Authors like Eve Bunting often develop their stories by reviewing the headlines in the newspaper. To understand this process, students can search the Internet or local newspaper for a story, either past or present, that piques their interest. Encourage them to do additional research to discover information that will support their own response to the story and to make it as accurate and authentic as possible. Then have them write, using a first-person perspective.

- *Author or Illustrator as Simile* After students have had an opportunity to read a number of books by the same author or illustrator and to explore the biographical information available about him, they are ready to create a simile. For example: "Eve Bunting is like gum because once she gets an idea she sticks to it."

- *Time Lines or Mapping* Both of these strategies assist listeners in creating a visual representation of the story's action, the critical events that occur, or the significant moments in a character's or individual's life.

- *Sketch Journals* Some students prefer to express their thoughts and connections through sketching rather than writing. Listeners in the read aloud experience should also have the opportunity to respond through music, drama, or movement. We are always amazed at how a story can generate a response using the fine arts.

Strategies for Supporting Literature Responses Through Discussion

It is imperative that students don't sit and listen to a story being read aloud without having the opportunity to discuss it. Discussions are key to assisting listeners in making meaning and interpretations that lead to personal connections. Some good strategies to support small- and whole-group discussions are:

- *Author or Illustrator Study* Use the read aloud experience to highlight the craft of a specific author or illustrator. By reading aloud a number of books written or illustrated by the same individual, students can begin to distinguish the writing style of the author and the topics the author may select. An illustrator study focuses on the artistic style and medium used to complement or extend the story. Share information about the author's or illustrator's life in conjunction with the read aloud. Make additional books available to encourage students to read independently as well. An excellent picture-author for older grades to study is Eve Bunting. Her books emphasize a variety of social issues:

A Train to Somewhere (orphan trains)

So Far from the Sea (Japanese internment)

The Wednesday Surprise (adult illiteracy)

Rudi's Pond (death)

The Sunshine Home (aging)

Fly Away Home and *December* (homelessness)

I Have an Olive Tree (family heritage)

A Picnic in October (immigration)

Smoky Night (Los Angeles riots)

- *Discussion Strategies* Before, during, and after the read aloud experience, it is important that students have an opportunity to discuss the story. Here are some strategies to support those discussions:

  1. *Chapter Chat* At particular points in a chapter or at the end of the chapter reading for the day or time, have students turn to a partner and chat about their connections to the story. This can also be done easily with a picture book. This strategy allows all students to discuss the story. The teacher may decide if and when the discussions are shared with another pair of listeners or with the whole class.

  2. *Discussion Perspective* Assign students a perspective that will determine how they discuss the book with others (or have them select a perspective that they feel strongly about in relation to the story). This strategy promotes both critical and creative thinking. Perspectives might include, but are not limited to: the synthesizer, who listens to everyone and synthesizes the responses at various points during the discussion; the optimist, who views everything in the story in a positive manner; the pessimist, who only sees the bad in every action of the character; the emotional responder, who reacts through anger, compassion, laughter, etc.; and the creative problem solver, who tries to find imaginative ways to deal with characters' dilemmas.

3. *Literature Circles* We often think of literature circles as something students participate in following their own independent reading. However, read alouds can serve the same purpose. Group students together in small clusters of four to six to discuss the story. They can use some of the same strategies to prepare for the discussion as they would if they were reading independently. These strategies might include journaling, writing down quotes from the book to discuss, jotting down personal connections, or indicating their overall impressions of the story and possible questions that they may have to share with the group. It is helpful to have additional copies of the book being read aloud for students to refer to as they prepare for and engage in literature circles.

These response strategies and discussion ideas are just a few of our favorites. They can all be adapted to support your read aloud experience and the students in your classroom.

8

Questioning Our Questions

Curiosity can't be forced. It must be awakened. Read, and trust the eyes that open slowly, the faces that light up, the questions that will begin to form and give way to other questions. The pathways to knowledge do not end in this classroom; they should start from it.

DANIEL PENNAC
Better Than Life

Teachers love to ask questions, especially after reading a book aloud to their students. Many teachers tell us that if they don't ask questions, either their students won't talk or they will never be sure whether their students understood the story. We know, however, that the types of questions we ask, when and how we ask them, and how students interpret them may have a tremendous effect on how students respond to the literature we share. Should we, as Pennac suggests in the opening epitaph, wait until students' questions begin to form and give way to other questions? Or do we need to ask them up front to be sure that students are attending to the things we feel they should attend to?

Several assumptions underlie traditional questioning techniques used by many classroom teachers before, during, and after reading aloud a piece of literature. First, it is assumed that particular meanings in a piece of literature are more important than other meanings, and that it is the teachers' job to know which is which and to see if students are getting the "correct" meanings. Most of us can remember sitting in high school English classes and college literature courses trying to "guess what was in the teacher's head." We learned that what we thought about a book wasn't as important as what the teacher thought. Because of this, we often turned to the Cliff Notes or other "authorities" to tell us what the story really meant and where the hidden meanings could be found. It is assumed that teachers know what students need to know about a book, and questions are the best way to find out if students have acquired the correct meanings.

Second, it is assumed that these correct meanings, or what we have traditionally referred to as "main ideas," are to be found *in* the text. There is *one* correct answer, and questions will be asked until students can be guided to deliver the correct interpretation. It is assumed that the best way to elicit students' ideas is through questioning, and that it is the teacher's job to ask these questions.

Finally, it is assumed that questions function more often as a classroom management technique than as a teaching strategy. When Frank's mother used to ask him, "Frank William Serafini Jr., what is all that noise in the kitchen?" he quickly learned that she really wasn't interested in what he was doing in the kitchen. She already knew. The question was used to let him know that she knew. Teachers often use questions the same way. "Is that how second graders respond to a story?" or, " Chandler, have we been paying attention?" or, "Morgan, can you tell me what just happened in the book?"

The types of questions we ask should be respectful of students' understandings and play an invitational role, rather than a managerial one. Asking questions is not inherently bad teaching. There are good questions to be asked, and appropriate times to ask them. However, we may need to reconsider how we use questions and for what purpose. This chapter presents a series of "considerations" to help teachers rethink the kinds of questions they ask, why they ask them, and what purpose asking questions should serve. We conclude with a set of instructional ideas designed to get teachers started toward changing their questioning practices.

Consideration #1: Questions should provide space for an acceptable range of answers, possibilities, and interpretations. The types of questions we ask should allow students to offer multiple ideas, not simply identify a single, predetermined main idea. Many ideas arise in transactions with literature. Our questions should open up discussions, not reduce them to a main-idea scavenger hunt.

Consideration #2: Questions should help readers make connections to their lives and other literary experiences. Making connections between what is being read and the events in our lives is an important part of being a reader. Literature is always grounded in the events of the world, and it is in this relationship that we learn about ourselves. Questions concerning what a particular book reminds us about—whether we have ever met a character like the one in the story, whether we would react the same way to the events in the story, and so on—help us create emotional and intellectual ties with the books we read.

Consideration #3: *Questions should promote further inquiry, discussion, and reflection.* We know there is a big difference between asking an open-ended question and a literal-recall question. Literal-recall questions force readers to attend only to what is presented in the book, leaving their transactions with the text and personal responses outside the conversation. When we ask literal-recall questions, there are correct answers. But who cares, for instance, what color Max's wolf suit was in *Where the Wild Things Are*? Is that really important to our interpretations of the story? We need to ask questions that elicit thinking and reflection, not memorization of textual elements. We don't want our questions to become a literary version of Trivial Pursuit.

Consideration #4: *Questions seem to be more effective when they are asked in response to students' ideas, rather than preempting them.* When we finish a book and allow students to make comments, we open up the discussion to those ideas that are important to them. When we begin this discussion by asking a particular question, we narrow the possibilities for students' response. We need to see what is important to our readers first, to learn what they want to talk about before we begin to ask questions. When we ask students questions in response to their responses, we help them clarify and expand their ideas and learning.

Consideration #5: *Asking too many questions, even good ones, can shut down a good discussion.* Teachers need to consider how many questions they ask and why they ask them. We recommend tape-recording some of your read aloud discussions during the year and listening to what happens. We have our graduate students in children's literature record and transcribe a read aloud experience each semester to see what is happening in their literature discussions. It is an eye-opening experience. As teachers, we need to be able to step back and understand our role during the read aloud experience. Playing Twenty Questions may be a good parlor game, but it is not sound instructional pedagogy.

Consideration #6: *Questions should have integrity. Teachers should not ask questions when they already know the answers.* When we begin asking questions we already know the answers to, we play the game of, Guess What's in My Head? These questions change the way students respond and the tenor of our conversations. Would we walk out of a movie with our friends and ask them, "What was the plot of the movie?" or "Who is the main character and why?" If there is some bit of information so important that every child must know it, make a statement, tell students what you want them to know, don't ask questions with predetermined answers. Students quickly learn that the teacher knows the answer, and that their personal ideas become secondary to finding the correct responses that the teacher has in mind.

Consideration #7: *Questions should help students explain or justify their ideas.* When we ask questions, we are actually providing an opportunity for students to offer text-based or experienced-based warrants for their interpretations. If we allow students to justify their ideas only by direct reference to the text, we negate their transactions with the story. On the other hand, if we allow students to offer any idea they want without providing evidence of their interpretations, the piece of literature is not respected. Students need to know that their ideas have to be grounded either in the text or in their experiences in the world. Evidence can come from either of these sources, but there must be a warrant for the interpretations readers construct. Questions can help students explain where and how these warrants are grounded.

Consideration #8: *Questions should help students notice things in the text and in their lives that they wouldn't notice on their own.* Some of the most effective types of questions we hear teachers use involve "calling to conscious attention" elements in the text and students' lives. Questions used to open up the discussion, to probe further into the literary experience and to develop more sophisticated transactions between reader and text are most effective. As literary docents, one of our main responsibilities is to help students see what is possible. We want to help them fully experience the literature we share and enjoy themselves in the process.

Suggestions for Using Questions

In addition to the above considerations, the following instructional ideas may help teachers to change their questioning techniques. First, we believe that students should be encouraged to ask more questions. It is important for readers to take an active stance during the reading process. One aspect of an active stance is to question what is presented in the books we read and how the events in the story relate to one's experiences. We want our students to question the world.

Second, we cannot assume that all readers ask good questions, or that the kinds of questions they ask go beyond literal recall. Students become socialized into particular ways of responding to texts in the course of their school career. Often, we need to help them learn to ask different types of questions and to talk about books in a new way (see Figure 8–1). By demonstrating the kinds of questions we should ask while we are reading, we may help readers adopt new perspectives concerning the literature they encounter.

Third, instead of asking questions, teachers can make statements about the literature being read. In our experience, we have found that statements elicit more responses from students than do questions. When we openly share our reactions and ideas, students learn to respond openly and honestly as well. We want students to tell us what they think and to feel comfortable sharing their ideas, whether those ideas are fully formed or half-baked. When students see us struggling to make sense of texts and sharing our best-guesses about a story, they learn that interpreting stories is not an easy process. Students also learn that some questions may not have immediate or definitive answers. This is part of the challenge as well as the excitement of reading.

Author and Text Based

What are some important ideas in the story?

What is the author trying to tell you?

How did the author describe the character?

What is the setting and plot of the story?

What is the main character like?

Reader Based

What do you think this story is about?

How did you feel as you read the story?

What connections (personal/literary) did you make as you were reading?

Do the characters remind you of anyone?

Can you relate to the challenges the characters faced? How so?

How would you have acted if you were the main character?

World Based

Are any of the characters privileged or marginalized?

What attitudes or worldviews are endorsed/diminished?

What assumptions are taken for granted?

How are critical issues (race, gender, class, ethnicity) dealt with?

Figure 8–1. Types of Questions

9
Sharing Informational and Chapter Books

Over the past decade, informational books have undergone the greatest transforma-
tion of all genres in children's literature. No longer do informational books contain
endless facts and boring illustrations. Instead, they present information in an interesting and exciting way while engaging readers' attention with stunning photographs
or eye-catching illustrations. Students' school library selections show that informational books are definitely the desired choice. So why aren't teachers selecting them
for reading aloud in the classroom?

The term *informational* rather than *nonfiction* is the one we prefer using in discussing books that contain informative text and illuminating illustrations. Nonfiction
includes poetry and plays as well as books that contain factual information. We are
focusing on those books that present information on various topics such as animals,
astronomy, the Middle Ages, or cooking. While we certainly support reading lots of
poetry, we have found that teachers often read poetry aloud, while informational
books are still the least likely to be selected for this purpose.

Could it be that many informational books published decades ago contain bland
writing, limited visual appeal, and sometimes inaccuracies in the information presented? Is it because teachers feel the books' format, with all of the captioned
illustrations, nonlinear text, and layout and design, does not lend itself to reading aloud

to students? Anyone who has ever tried to read a Magic School Bus book in one sitting will certainly attest to the difficulty of keeping students engaged while reading the story line, speech balloons, and factual information contained in the sidebars. These types of books can be read aloud, but possibly there are some different strategies for doing so.

In the past, informational books have had a place in the elementary- and middle-grade curriculums, but more as supporting rather than primary materials. When units of study begin, teachers often request that the school librarian locate numerous books on a particular topic. These books are then placed in the classroom as resources, balanced along the chalk tray for student perusal, or set up in a center or study area.

But reading aloud informational books can inform readers about a given topic and also whet their appetite to continue reading independently about the subject. Even the most reluctant reader can get excited about informational books because they are often more accessible and don't have to be read from cover to cover. Readers can develop strategies for reading informational books independently because similar strategies have been modeled by the teacher during the read aloud experience.

Just as some picture books do not lend themselves to reading aloud, certain informational books are not suited to this experience. There are five A's to consider when evaluating the quality of an informational book:

1. ***Authority of the author*** Is the author an authority on the topic or has he consulted with experts in that field?

2. ***Accuracy of the text*** Misinformation is sometimes worse than no information. The factual information contained in the text, illustrations, diagrams, charts, graphs, and so on should be accurate. Sometimes the best research projects evolve when conflicting information is presented through various resources and students embark on discovering what is truly factual.

3. ***Appropriateness for students*** Teachers in intermediate and middle school grades should select books whose text is interesting and flows well during reading aloud. If the text contains too many scientific terms that are beyond or impede student comprehension, then it may not be the best choice.

4. ***Artistry*** Many informational books are written in a narrative style using similes, metaphors, and visual imagery. Listeners don't want to hear endless facts read, but want information that piques their interest and engages them.

5. ***Appearance of the book*** Various formats, fonts, and features highlight the appearance of informational books. Text is broken up with numerous captioned illustrations, charts, graphs, maps, boxed facts, and other aspects that make the book visually appealing. Information about topics such as grammar may appear in a pop-up format, pages may fold out to reveal a scaled version of a blue whale, or fascinating borders may contain additional information or visual elements that complement or extend the text.

Once the book is selected, teachers should spend some time planning and pre-reading. As with other read alouds, there should be a curricular connection. Teachers may need to present some background information before reading aloud. The book should be read previously to make sure that technical terms are understood and pronounced correctly and that questions supporting the read aloud experience can be asked (and answered). It may not be appropriate to read the entire book. The teacher may elect instead to read portions of the book over several days or read only those pages that are relevant to the study. Decisions about reading components of the book such as captions will also need to be determined.

To enhance the curriculum, teachers might want to read several informational books about the same topic, such as the Civil War, or numerous books by the same author, such as James Cross Giblin, Russell Freedman, or Gail Gibbons, to observe how they present information in their books. Informational books might support a fiction book selection by adding insight into the way an author weaves in facts, such as in *Number the Stars* by Lois Lowry, and accompanying this by sharing books aloud about the Danish Resistance.

Informational books are compelling and provide another approach for presenting facts. Nonfiction books receive recognition through the National Council of Teachers of English Orbis Pictus Award and the American Library Association's Sibert Informational Book Award. This distinction indicates that informational books are valuable literary works that should be a part of every classroom's read aloud experience.

Reading Chapter Books Aloud

The majority of *Reading Aloud and Beyond* has focused on reading aloud picture books to older students. Picture books can often be read in one sitting, often contain text that naturally lends itself to being read aloud, and often present exquisite illustrations to capture listeners' attention. Chapter books or novels have generally been those texts that teachers select for reading aloud in intermediate and middle school classrooms. Many times chapter books are used as a classroom management tool after lunch to quiet students before moving on to subjects such as math or science; read while students are busy finishing up class assignments; or utilized as a time filler at the end of the day. They usually aren't discussed or responded to in any way and may not even be connected to the curriculum. Reading a chapter book aloud is an investment of time over several weeks. Shouldn't it support and generate the curriculum?

At the beginning of each school year, Cyndi carefully selects a chapter book to read aloud that would set the tone for the rest year. This was the book that students would make constant references to and that provided a shared experience around which to build the classroom community. It also provided the foundation for the unit of study that would be continued in some aspects throughout the year.

One successful chapter book read aloud is *Because of Winn-Dixie* by Kate DiCamillo. Opal Buloni has just moved to a small Florida town with her preacher father. On her first trip to the Winn-Dixie grocery store, Opal encounters a mangy-looking dog who is creating havoc in the produce section. Opal claims the dog is hers and when questioned about the dog's name she states what immediately comes to mind—Winn-Dixie. This engaging book contains well-written, appealing text that flows from chapter to chapter, promoting numerous opportunities for class discussions. The theme of creating community naturally evolves from the book and can help teachers develop a sense of classroom community as well.

While reading this book, Cyndi also generates text sets, or groups of books, to be read and discussed by small groups of students. Some of the text sets focus on the following ideas: what community is, changes in community, community challenges, diverse communities, communities of the past, connecting to communities, defining community, and building community. For example, in the "what community is" text set, picture books about different communities were presented; for example, New York City, in a *It's a Dog's New York* by Susan L. Roth; a neighborhood, in *Madlenka's Dog* by Peter Sis or *Everybody Brings Noodles* by Norah Dooley; an apartment building, in *Mama Provi and the Pot Rice* by Sylvia Rosa-Casanova; a Ugandan village, in *Beatrice's Goat* by Page McBrier; and a school community, portrayed in *Thank you, Mr. Falker* by Patricia Polacco or *It's a Fine, Fine School* by Sharon Creech. The stories in this text set extend the discussion and allow students to make powerful connections to *Because of Winn-Dixie*. These books also support various perspectives about community while generating questions that led to the next unit of study.

Just as with picture books, it is critical that teachers preread the chapter book to familiarize themselves with the content of the book and how it supports the curriculum, and to plan ways to promote student discussion and, possibly, anticipate listeners' questions. While prereading a chapter book, teachers will also discover natural places to end the reading for the day. Time shouldn't determine how long a book is read; rather, teachers should acknowledge natural stopping places within the book that will create suspense for the next time, generate student response, and provide strategies for extending the curriculum.

Reading aloud chapter books also enables listeners to create their own visual images about the characters' appearance, the story setting, and the situations or events that protagonists encounter. Students' visual response to a novel gives teachers an insight into their personal connections to the story. Many chapter books have been made into videos or movies. Sometimes it is interesting to view these visual representations following the reading of a chapter book to see not only how the actors portraying the characters look but also to compare the movie adaptation of the novel.

Most adults, if asked, could relate a memory about a book that was read aloud to them by a teacher or parent. Reading aloud establishes community within a classroom through shared experience and literary connections. Students will continue to connect to these books long after the physical act of reading has been completed. This in turn will, we believe, promote lifelong readers.

10

Evaluating Responses to Literature

Despite occasional brilliant studies, researchers thus far have only a limited understanding of the complex dimensions of reader response.

ALAN PURVES AND V. RIPPERE
Elements of Writing About a Literary Work

Assessing the responses that readers construct to the literature they encounter is as complex as the reading process itself, and is often done for the wrong reasons. Using standardized tests to determine a reader's grade level does not help classroom teachers support students' development as a reader, nor does it help readers construct more sophisticated responses to the literature being shared during a read aloud. Traditional, standardized assessment has very little to do with teaching and learning, and more to do with making comparisons across large populations of readers. Like standardized tests, most commercial forms of reading assessment take place after the reading event and are used to determine the effectiveness of a readers' renditions or understandings of a particular text at a particular time and place.

In many ways, assessing readers' responses to literature falls into this trap. Traditional tests and quizzes don't assess a readers' lived-through experience or immediate reactions like laughing, smiling, or crying. These immediate, unrehearsed responses to the literature we read aloud provide us with an important window into our students' response strategies. Even most basal program teacher's manuals acknowledge the complexity of the reading process by declaring that "answers may vary."

Before we wrote this book, we considered whether we even wanted to talk about assessment. We felt that there was too much focus on assessment in our educational publications and institutions. What could we say that hadn't already been said or that would make a difference for teachers and students? On the other hand, recent legislation and mandates from the federal and state departments of education were forcing teachers to attend to assessment more than they wanted, which meant that they would need some ideas about how to assess readers' abilities. So we decided to include in this chapter methods for gathering information and assessing that inform teachers' instructional decisions and the learning experiences they create.

As we read aloud with our students, we listen carefully to the ways they respond and the interpretations they construct. We watch how they listen to and talk to each other. We collect information by listening to students' ideas, having them respond in writing, or having them think aloud during their readings. Once information has been collected, we need criteria to evaluate students' development as readers and interpreters of literature. This is where things get a bit more complicated.

When talking to students about the books we have read aloud and listening to their responses, teachers often make judgments about whether a child has "gotten it." Our question has become, "Gotten what?" When we predetermine the understandings and the responses that children should have, we end up assessing their alignment to our responses, not what is important about their responses. As readers of literature, we will have ideas about what a text means, but our assessment needs to be an inquiry into the students' responses, not ours. We need to examine the growing complexity and sophistication of their ideas, not their alignment to our predetermined meanings. When we adopt a reader-based perspective (or a reader- *and* text-based perspective, as Rosenblatt suggests) rather than a text-based perspective, simple definitions of reading comprehension become more problematic. Assessing whether students have "gotten it" may lead us in the wrong direction.

The most basic assessment of a reader's response is whether a student can recall elements from a text. Multiple-choice questions like those found in many Informal Reading Inventories and computer-based assessments (for example, Accelerated Reader) focus on the reader's ability to recall exact language or events. We don't believe these assessments are effective in understanding students' responses to literature. By focusing on literal recall and a student's ability to remember exact words in a text, we are privileging the role of the text in the act of reading and dismissing the role played by the reader in transaction with the text. In doing so, we may be sending the wrong message to students about what is important in the process of reading. Our assessments should focus on, and align with, those processes and responses we want students to develop.

Margaret Meek (1988) has suggested that one of our primary responsibilities as educators is to find ways to make students' literate abilities visible. What assessments can we use to help our students' abilities to come forth? The first challenge of classroom-based assessment is to find ways of gathering and recording information, the second is to find ways to analyze or evaluate what has been collected.

Gathering Information

By listening to students' responses, talking with them about their readings, and reading through their literature response logs, we are able to gather information concerning students' responses to texts and their reading abilities. Using observational records (we prefer notebooks or computer labels), we write down things we observe, to reflect on later. Since we are reading aloud when these discussions take place, we can't always record our observations as they happen. We suggest taking a few moments as close to the read aloud time as possible to record observations. The closer to the event, the better the observational record.

Another way to gather information is to audio- or videotape some of your read aloud sessions. Although we would not do this every day, or even every week, recording at least one read aloud each semester helped us become better at reading aloud and promoting invested discussions. This technology enabled us to step back from our roles as reader and discussion facilitator to observe how we interacted during the read aloud experience. The tapes became an invaluable learning experience.

If we had an assistant, student teacher, or intern in our class, we sometimes asked him to read aloud so we could watch our students, or we asked him to make observations. Use whatever means is available to gather information during the read aloud session.

We also gather information though students' written responses to texts. Students' literature response logs provide us with information about students' individual responses. Frank used to use what he called a "walking journal" to record whole class responses. After reading a particular book, he would write something in a notebook and then "walk" it over to one of his students, who would then write her response to what he had written. After responding in the journal, the student would pass the walking journal to another student, and so on. This notebook became an interesting artifact for examining readers' responses to the books that had been shared aloud.

The biggest challenge for teachers is what to do with the information once it has been gathered. Developing a set of criteria that can be used to evaluate the information we have collected is the focus of the rest of this chapter.

Criteria for Evaluating Reader Response

In general, the different criteria that researchers have developed are based on a hierarchy or categorization scheme that extends along a continuum from literal response, or the ability to retell a story, to more complex analyses of elements and structures of a piece of literature. The various hierarchies and categories offered by researchers differ in the number of levels presented and how each level is defined.

Marjorie Hancock (2000) describes three primary categories—Immersion, Self-Involvement, and Detachment—with several secondary categories. These categories suggest a range from reader engagement with text to critical, objective analyses of literature. Sam Sebesta, Dianne Monson, and Helene Senn (1995) offer a hierarchical response to literature that ranges from efferent responses, which involve the ability to recall exact elements of the text, to evaluative responses, which involve evaluations of the quality of a piece of literature.

Based on the work of these researchers and others, we have constructed criteria to evaluate a reader's response to literature. Our criteria is organized around three modes of response rather than as a hierarchy of responses. We see these three modes as various perspectives that readers can adopt during the transaction with a text. More proficient readers are able to respond across all three modes, rather than focus on any one. It is a reader's ability to adopt multiple stances, multiple ways of responding to texts, that suggests their level of reading competence. We have designed the three modes as a heuristic device or checklist that teachers can use to organize and evaluate the information they have gathered about a particular student's responses (see Figure 10–1).

Although these modes of response may seem to range from simplistic to complex, we view them as different ways of responding, not different levels of response. When classroom instruction focuses on literal recall of texts and retelling stories, and does not support other modes of response, students learn to offer only those responses supported in the classroom. By encouraging other modes of response, we can support students in their development of associative and evaluative response-abilities. The expectations we construct in our community of readers affects the types of response we will get from students. This should not surprise us.

In many ways, the assessments we use to gather and evaluate students' responses will give us insights into the community of readers we have developed. If we want students to respond in ways other than recalling exact language from a text, we have to demonstrate those response modes and support students adopting those ways of talking about literature. It's as much about changing the way we talk about texts as it is about teaching children how to read literature.

Engaged/Involved

- can retell story
- is able to enter the imaginary world of a story
- relives the experience of the story
- offers immediate reactions (laughs, worries, etc.)
- can describe visual images created during the reading
- anticipates events next in the story; predicts
- follows along with a character's actions and decisions
- recalls specific events, language, and details from the story

Associative/Intertextual

- makes connections to other stories and texts
- makes connections to personal experiences
- relates story to events in the world
- understands challenges the characters face
- puts self in characters' place; offers suggestions

Reflective/Evaluative

- evaluates characters' motives
- see relationship between parts of a story and story as a whole
- evaluates quality of story
- infers author's intentions
- develops themes
- generalizes from literary experiences to life's experiences
- metacognitive; analyzes own responses to texts
- adopts critical and pragmatic perspectives
- reexamines own worldviews
- examines internal coherence of story
- evaluates the relevance of story to one's life

Figure 10–1. Reader Response Evaluation Criteria

11

Generating Curriculum

John Patrick Norman McHennessey set off along the road to learn.

JOHN BURNINGHAM
John Patrick Norman McHennessey

I (Frank) recently ordered a paperback copy of one of my favorite picture books enti-
tled *John Patrick Norman McHennessy-the boy who was always late*, by John
Burningham, from a book-supply warehouse. I wanted to share this humorous story—
about a boy who tells imaginative tales about his exploits on the way to school, only
to have his teacher not believe him and punish him for lying—with my undergradu-
ate children's literature students. When the book arrived, I opened it to enjoy by
myself once again before going to class. I was immediately dismayed, even angered, to
find a set of literal comprehension questions, a series of writing prompts, and other
assorted "enrichment activities" printed on the inside of the front and back covers.

Inside the front cover there was a note to parents and teachers, written by the
new publisher (Dragonfly) of the paperback edition. The note indicated that the publisher had included two pages of activities to use with students or children who were
"inspired by the story." In addition to a set of five literal-recall questions, there were
several writing prompts, an art activity, and directions for playing a game based on
the events of the story. I was appalled that the publisher had included these in the
book. I had not intended on buying a teaching guide for the book. I wanted the story,
not some scripted lessons. Usually, these teaching guides are offered by publishers
only at literacy conferences or in the back of particular literacy journals. They can be
avoided or purchased, as the teacher chooses. This time they came prepackaged with
the book. I was livid!

The included activities were superficially related to the story and ridiculous at best. One activity asked students to think up pretend reasons for being late and include a real one and a fake one, then see if their friends could guess which was which.

In my children's literature class at the university, I shared some of the challenges these activities created for me. A student pointed out that another publisher (Scholastic) included "literature circle questions" in a separate section at the end of the book *Stargirl* by Jerry Spinelli. This powerful young-adult novel tells the story of an eccentric high school girl who rejects the status quo and behaves in ways that confuse and astound her classmates. Stargirl is befriended by a boy named Leo, and their budding romance and the challenges presented to Leo by dating Stargirl are the focus of much of the story. The publisher wrote in the directions that these questions would help students "get more out of the experience of reading *Stargirl*." The publisher further indicated that these questions were "keyed" to Bloom's Taxonomy. Also included were several activities and projects that were suggested for use when the students finished reading the book.

We begin to feel nervous about the words *activities* and *projects* when they are being used to describe the kinds of prescribed experiences publishers were including with children's literature. One project directed students to make up fake greeting cards to give to fellow students like Stargirl did in the novel. Another had them creating an inauthentic speech for a staged speaking contest like the one Stargirl experienced in the story.

I immediately went to find Cyndi to share my experience and my concerns. She was equally appalled. This led to a wonderful discussion about the kinds of experiences we would and would not require or suggest before, during, or after reading a book with our students. We discussed the characteristics of a quality response experience with read alouds. What was it about the activities that the publishers included in those two books that bothered us so? Why did these experiences not align with our beliefs and teaching practices? As we set out to find some answers to these questions, we realized that this was really the focus of everything we believe about reading aloud and responding to literature.

Generating Curriculum with Read Alouds

One of the reasons we were so appalled at the low-level questions and simplistic activities that were suggested for students to engage in after reading these stories is that we had previously shared both *John Patrick Norman McHennessy-the boy who was always late* and *Stargirl* with students at a variety of grade levels who recognized the incredible story within each book. Those students' comments, questions, and personal connections were meaningful to them and reflected their ability to go beyond a superficial level of understanding to a deeper layer of insight and an appreciation for these creative books.

As we have stated previously, the books chosen for reading aloud in the traditional classroom are not always those the teacher uses to generate curriculum. At best they may support the curriculum, but often don't lead to bigger ideas that produce the next units of study. There are also times when a teacher may not recognize how to generate curriculum from the read aloud.

Stargirl by Jerry Spinelli is a particularly compelling book for intermediate- and middle-level grade students. Stargirl Caraway marches to the beat of her own drum. Her fellow classmates offer various theories as to her origins: "She was an alien. She was homeschooling gone amok. Her parents were circus acrobats. Her parents were witches" (2000, 14). Of course, none of these theories are true and the students at Mica Area High School realize that Stargirl is as real and as genuine as they are not. What makes *Stargirl* so powerful are the characterizations and the likelihood that adolescents may see themselves and their own behavior within the story—whether it is in the free-spirited Stargirl, her shy and conforming love interest, the school outcasts, the cheerleaders, or just one of the kids in the crowd who doesn't want to stand out too much or for the wrong reasons. Throughout the story, typical adolescent personalities are represented. Students may connect to one of these characters or to the situations depicted in the novel. This all leads to meaningful small-group and whole-class discussions.

An effective strategy for generating curriculum is to have students write down *topics, issues,* and *questions* related to the book during and after reading aloud *Stargirl*. Possible topics might be friendship, the issue may be how friendships are formed, or Why do some people have a lot of friends and others don't? Form small groups of four or five students so that they can periodically discuss their topics, issues, and questions.

At the end of *Stargirl* each student in the group should read their topics, issues, and questions to their peers. It works better if each topic, issue, and question is written on a separate piece of paper that can be grouped together and also moved around. After all the students organize the pieces of paper under topics, issues, and questions they then group together the ones they believe are similar across all three. Every topic, issue, and question must be placed in a pile or group. The students then name the grouping or category they have created. Once all of the student groups have completed this process (which may take several days and lots of discussion), each group shares their category names with the whole class while the teacher writes them on the chalkboard for everyone to see. Some of the categories we have generated with students from *Stargirl* are: individuality, achievements, environment/nature, the arts, culture, school, and peer relationships. These categories are broad enough that the teacher can incorporate mandated curriculum yet also find creative methods to approach curriculum that is relevant and meaningful for students. The important point to remember is that all aspects of the curriculum connect back to *Stargirl* because that is where they were generated. The next read aloud can then support one of these categories and continue to generate curriculum.

Another strategy for generating curriculum is to create text sets that relate to the book being read aloud. For example, after reading *John Patrick Norman McHennessy-the boy who was always late*, students can continue their reading through text sets. Again, using small groups of students, have them read the books in each text set and web out their ideas and connections. Some of the text sets we have generated in the past relating to *John Patrick Norman McHennessey* are:

Memorable Teachers

Finchler, Judy. 2000. *Testing Miss Malarkey.* Ill. Kevin O'Malley. Upper Saddle River, NJ: Walker.

Hill, Kirkpatrick. 2000. *The Year of Miss Agnes.* New York: Simon & Schuster.

Houston, Gloria. 1992. *My Great Aunt Arizona.* Ill. Susan Condie Lamb. New York: HarperCollins.

Morgenstern, Susie. 2001. *A Book of Coupons.* Ill. Serge Bloch. New York: Viking.

Polacco, Patricia. 1998. *Thank You, Mr. Falker!* New York: Philomel.

School Experiences

Clements, Andrew. 2002. *Jake Drake, Class Clown.* New York: Simon & Schuster.

Gantos, Jack. 1998. *Joey Pigza Swallowed a Key.* New York: Farrar, Straus & Giroux.

Littlesugar, Amy. 2001. *Freedom School, Yes!* Ill. Floyd Cooper. New York: Philomel.

Lorbiecki, Maribeth. 1998. *Sister Anne's Hands.* Ill. Wendy Popp. New York: Dial Books.

Medina, Jane. 1999. *My Name is Jorge: On Both Sides of the River: Poems in English and Spanish.* Ill. Fabricio Vanden Broeck. Honesdale, PA: Boyds Mills.

Perez, L. King. 2002. *First Day in Grapes.* Ill. Robert Casilla. New York: Lee & Low.

Books Written and/or Illustrated by John Burningham

Burningham, John. 1971. *Mr. Gumpy's Outing*. New York: Holt.

Burningham, John. 1983. *Come Away from the Water Shirley*. New York: Crowell.

Burningham, John. 1987. *Granpa*. New York: Crown.

Burningham, John. 1991. *Hey! Get off Our Train*. New York: Crown.

Fleming, Ian. *Chitty Chitty Bang Bang. The Magical Car*. 1994. Ill. John Burningham. New York: Random House.

Reality Mixed with Fantasy

Falconer, Ian. 2001. *Olivia Saves the Circus*. New York: Simon & Schuster.

Kenah, Katharine. 2000. *The Dream Shop*. Ill. Peter Catalanotto. New York: HarperCollins.

Sendak, Maurice. 1963. *Where the Wild Things Are*. New York: Harper & Row.

Wiesner, David. 1999. *Sector 7*. New York: Clarion.

Yorinks, Arthur. 2001. *Company's Going*. Ill. David Small. New York: Hyperion.

Yorinks, Arthur. 1986. *Hey, Al!* Ill. Richard Egielski. New York: Farrar, Straus & Giroux.

People Who View the World in Different Ways

Blos, Joan. 1990. *Old Henry*. Ill. Stephen Gammell. New York: Morrow.

Fleischman, Paul. 1999. *Weslandia*. Ill. Kevin Hawkes. Cambridge, MA: Candlewick.

Grimes, Nikki. 2002. *Talkin' About Bessie*. Ill. E. B. Lewis. New York: Orchard.

Kerley, Barbara. 2001. *The Dinosaurs of Waterhouse Hawkins*. Ill. Brian Selznick. New York: Scholastic.

Raschka, Chris. 2002. *John Coltrane's Giant Steps*. New York: Atheneum.

Rubin, Susan Goldman. 2001. *The Yellow House*. Ill. Jos. A. Smith. New York: Abrams.

Vignette Texts with Repeating Lines or Phrases

Baylor, Byrd. 1978. *The Other Way to Listen*. Ill. Peter Parnall. New York: Scribner's.

Laminack, Lester. 1998. *The Sunsets of Miss Olivia Wiggins*. Ill. Constance Rummel Bergum. Atlanta, GA: Peachtree.

MacLachlan, Patricia. 1994. *All the Places to Love*. Ill. Mike Wimmer. New York: HarperCollins.

Rylant, Cynthia. 1982. *When I Was Young in the Mountains*. Ill. Diane Goode. New York: Dutton.

Weatherford, Carole Boston. 2000. *The Sound That Jazz Makes*. Ill. Eric Velasquez. New York: Walker.

Wiles, Deborah. 2001. *Love, Ruby Lavender*. San Diego, CA: Harcourt.

These text sets contain both picture and chapter books that work well for readers at the intermediate and middle school level who are at various reading abilities. The students do not need to read all of the books but should read several in the set so that they are not presenting their ideas but rather discussing them. This is critical because the books in a text set are related in some way and reading several allows students to discover the connections between their books and others' books. Once students have read and discussed the books in their text set, they can select another set to read and discuss, and create a web to represent their understandings. The next group can add to the existing web or begin one of their own. Then all of the webs are shared with the class, and the teacher assists students in determining the connections as well as relevant ideas or topics to pursue further.

Both of these strategies work well with intermediate- and middle-level students because they give students a voice in units of study that are part of the curriculum. When students feel they have a voice in what will be studied, they are much more engaged in the learning process. No longer is curriculum being done *to* students but rather *with* students. These processes also highlight the role and importance of the read aloud and its significance, not simply as part of the curriculum, but as key to the curriculum.

12

Where Do We Go from Here?

*If you have to ask yourself where you'll find the time, it means
the desire isn't there. Because if you look at it more carefully,
no one has the time to read, life [and school] is a perpetual plot
to keep us from reading.*

DANIEL PENNAC
Better Than Life

What good is it to present instructional techniques for reading aloud with students if teachers don't feel they have time to include them in their daily schedules? We understand that the curriculum in our schools has expanded at an exponential rate, with more and more special topics to be "covered" every year. But teachers, we have learned, include things in their daily and weekly schedules that they value the most. Curriculum, our lesson plan books, and our daily schedules are all value statements. We include in our schedules those things upon which we place the most importance. Classroom teachers have to learn to value and appreciate the instructional opportunities that reading aloud can contribute before they will include reading aloud in their classrooms on a daily basis.

We want the reading aloud and the sharing of literature in elementary, middle, and high school classrooms to become a daily ritual, a formalized habit. We want teachers to see reading aloud as an important element of reading instruction, not just a classroom management technique. We began this book with our own reasons for including reading aloud in the reading curriculum, but we know, ultimately, it is up to classroom teachers to decide whether to read aloud each and every day. Reading aloud with students should become such a vital part of the classroom that a day without a read aloud would feel awkward and incomplete. The sharing of literature brings us together as human beings, fills our souls, and revitalizes our desire to connect to others and our world through story.

Becoming invested in classroom discussions about literature, what Peterson and Eeds (1990) called "Grand Conversations," does not happen overnight. Students need time and support to learn new ways to talk about books, listen to other students, and share their feelings and ideas about the stories they hear. Because we know it takes time to develop the types of interactions around books that we have described, we offer the following ideas as places to start, as ways to begin to enhance the read aloud experience in your classroom.

1. *Increase your knowledge of children's literature*. In the opening section of Frank's book, *The Reading Workshop: Creating Space for Readers* (2001), he described how he spent his Saturday mornings wandering around the bookstore near his house. Going to a bookstore and browsing through the children's section or going to the local library to see what new books have arrived provided an opportunity to extend his knowledge of children's literature. With the overwhelming numbers of children's books published each year, we have all we can do to keep up with the quality literature being created. If we want grand conversations we need to read grand literature. If we want to read grand literature, we need to extend our knowledge base about what has been published.

2. *Read aloud every day for one month*. Give it a try. Pay attention to the way your students respond to what has been read. Listen to their comments and take notes about what you are hearing. We have learned that it takes time to develop a community of readers that are able to respond deeply to the literature we share with them. It will take about a month to begin to see a significant change in the way students respond to our new teaching practices. Throughout their time in schools, students have been initiated into particular ways of responding to stories. If the students in your classroom have only been asked to answer literal-recall questions, it will take time to help them change their ways of responding and begin to share their impressions, connections, and wonderings.

3. *Share literature at your staff meetings*. Teachers need help getting exposed to literature themselves. Principals that I have worked with have shared literature at staff meetings and during inservice workshops. In one school, we displayed books we were reading in our classrooms on a poster outside our classroom doors so that every class that walked by knew what we had been reading. This helps develop a community of readers across the school, not just within particular classrooms.

4. Share resources with parents. Parents are a child's first teacher. Many of them are looking for ways to help their child succeed. We need to be sure that children are being read to from birth, not just when they enter our classrooms. Providing readings lists, tips for reading aloud and discussing books, and resources for extending students' experiences with texts should be made available for parents.

5. Try some invested discussion ideas. Getting students to say more than, "I Liked the Book!" takes time and support. We have offered many strategies in this book to help you get students talking about books. Give some of them a try.

6. Get involved in literature studies yourself. Teachers need to know how to talk about books themselves before they can facilitate discussions with their students. We cannot assume that teachers, like students, will be able to begin grand conversations on their own. In our university classes, we require preservice teachers to read and discuss children's and young-adult novels in literature discussion groups. We know teachers may not have had opportunities to share their own ideas about literature before this. Before we are able to help students make richer connections and more sophisticated interpretations, we need to be able to do it ourselves.

7. Try thinking aloud. One of the best ways we know for demonstrating the kinds of impressions, connections, and wonderings (ways of thinking) we want students to engage in is through thinking aloud in front of students as we read with them. Think alouds are an instructional practice where a teacher reads a book and stops intermittently to share their thinking "aloud" with students. This sharing helps students learn how proficient readers make sense of the stories they read. It is through the unpacking of our thinking as successful readers that students learn how to read in more engaging ways themselves.

8. Rethink the notion of "Main Idea." As long as we believe that there is only one main idea, and that it resides *in* the text, our discussions will rarely progress past a scavenger hunt for the idea that is contained in the teacher's manual or the teacher's head. When we allow for multiple interpretations, multiple perspectives, we open up the discussion for students to offer their ideas. There isn't one main idea that resides in the text. As readers, we bring a variety of experiences and cultural histories to each text we read, and it is through our transactions with texts that meanings are constructed. What we need to do is create a space around our read alouds where students can share and negotiate the meanings they construct with the books we read with them.

9. *Revisit requisite reading skills.* For many years, basal reading programs have published a scope and sequence of the skills that students were required to learn throughout the instructional program. These skills included the ability to compare and contrast, sequencing, the ability to differentiate between fact and opinion, recognizing elements of literature, identifying the main idea, and the ability to literally recall events from the story. The skills that are needed in the literature-based classrooms we have described in this book may go well beyond the ones included in commercial reading programs. As classroom teachers, we need to revisit the skills we want students to develop to be sure they include those strategies and response-abilities that we are teaching.

10. *Understand the complex nature of the reading process.* Reading, as a meaning-making event, is a complex process that involves the orchestration of a variety of skills and strategies. If we go looking for a "silver bullet" program or professional development workshop that will solve all of our literacy challenges, we are denying this complexity, and allowing others to tell us what to do as teachers. It takes time, support, and opportunity to develop literate human beings. Reading aloud with students is just one part of a comprehensive reading framework, albeit an indispensable aspect as far as we are concerned.

We hope that these ten ideas will help you find your way into a literature-based classroom that is built upon the foundation of reading aloud with children. Becoming an experienced and effective teacher takes time and support. Teachers are more successful when they are able to work with other teachers who are struggling with the same issues and to find time to discuss the challenges they encounter. Find other, like-minded teachers that you feel comfortable talking with and share your ideas, challenges, and successes. Celebrate the growth you have made as teachers. It is important to recognize that teachers develop expertise over time in the company of other teachers and students.

We shall end our book with a quote by Margery Williams (1922) from the classic children's book *The Velveteen Rabbit*. This quote symbolizes the processes we go through as teachers. It is our hope that our book will provide the support and insights you need to become a better teacher and a better human being.

"It doesn't happen all at once," said the Skin Horse. "You become. It takes a long time. That's why it doesn't often happen to people who break easily, or have sharp edges, or who have to be carefully kept. Generally, by the time you are Real, most of your fur has been rubbed off, and your eyes drop out and you get loose in the joints and very shabby. But these things don't matter at all, because once you are Real you can't be ugly, except to people who don't understand."

Appendix A
Frank's 25 Favorite Illustrators

Graeme Base

Anthony Browne

John Burningham

Rod Clements

David Diaz

Leo and Diane Dillon

Kevin Henkes

William Joyce

Leo Lionni

David Macauley

David McPhail

Peter Parnall

Robert San Souci

Maurice Sendak

David Shannon

Peter Sis

Lane Smith

William Steig

Shaun Tan

Colin Thompson

Chris Van Allsburg

Julie Vivas

David Wiesner

David Wisniewski

Ed Young

Appendix B
Frank's 25 Favorite Authors

Avi

Natalie Babbitt

Eve Bunting

Aidan Chambers

Andrew Clements

Sharon Creech

Gary Crew

Christopher Paul Curtis

Roald Dahl

Jean Craighead George

Margaret Peterson Haddix

E. L. Konigsburg

Madeline L'Engle

Helen Lester

Lois Lowry

Patricia MacLachlan

John Marsdan

Scott O'Dell

Katherine Paterson

Gary Paulsen

Richard Peck

Phillip Pullman

Cynthia Rylant

Jerry Spinelli

Mildred Taylor

Appendix C
Cyndi's 25 Favorite Authors

Avi

Joseph Bruchac

Eve Bunting

Sharon Creech

Karen Cushman

Kate DiCamillo

Paul Fleischman

Mem Fox

Russell Freedman

Patricia Reilly Giff

Jan Greenberg and Sandra Jordan

Karen Hesse

Will Hobbs

Kimberly Willis Holt

Lois Lowry

Pat Mora

Walter Dean Myers

Donna Jo Napoli

Naomi Shihab Nye

Doreen Rappaport

Susan Goldman Rubin

Gary Soto

Sarah Stewart

Jacqueline Woodson

Jane Yolen

Appendix D
Cyndi's 25+ Favorite Illustrators

Anthony Browne

Peter Catalanotto

David Catrow

R. Gregory Christie

Bryan Collier

Barbara Cooney

Floyd Cooper

David Diaz

Lois Ehlert

Gail Gibbons

Kevin Hawkes

Kevin Henkes

Steven Kellogg

Betsy Lewin

E. B. Lewis

Robert McCloskey

Brian Pinkney

Chris Raschka

Synthia Saint James

Brian Selznick

Marc Simont

David Small

Diane Stanley

Simms Taback

Chris Van Allsburg

Rosemary Wells

David Wiesner

David Wisniewski

Don Wood

Appendix E
Frank's Current Top 25 Picture Books

Babbit, N. 1994. *Bub, or the Very Best* Thing. New York: HarperCollins.

Bloom, B. 1999. *Wolf!* Ill. Pascal Biet. New York: Orchard.

Browne, A. 1986. *Piggybook*. New York: Knopf.

Browne, A. 1998. *Voices in the Park*. New York: DK.

Bunting, E. 1994. *Night of the Gargoyles*. Ill. David Wiesner. Boston, MA: Clarion.

Coleman, E. 1996. *White Socks Only*. Ill. Tyrone Geter. Morton Grove, IL: Albert Whitman.

Crew, G. 1994. *The Watertower*. Ill. Steven Woolman. Flinders Park, SA, Australia: Era.

Fox, M. 1997. *The Straight Line Wonder*. Ill. Paul Rosenthal. New York: Mondo.

Fleischman, P. 1999. *Weslandia*. Ill. Kevin Hawkes. Boston, MA: Candlewick Press.

Goss, L., and C. Jabar. 1996. *The Frog Who Wanted to Be a Singer*. New York: Orchard.

Joyce, W. 1990. *A Day with Wilbur Robinson*. New York: HarperTrophy.

Lorbiecki, M. 1998. *Sister Anne's Hands*. Ill. Wendy Popp. New York: Dial Books.

Marsden, J. 1998. *The Rabbits*. Ill. Shaun Tan. Melbourne, Australia: Lothian.

McKissack, P. 1986. *Flossie and the Fox*. Ill. Rachel Isadora. New York: Dial Books for Young Readers.

McPhail, D. 1997. *Edward and the Pirates*. New York: Little, Brown.

Morrison, T. 1999. *The Big Box*. Ill. Giselle Potter. New York: Hyperion/Jump at the Sun.

Paz, O. 1997. *My Life with the Wave*. Trans. C. Cowan. Ill. Marc Buehner. New York: Lothrop, Lee & Shepard.

Rylant, C. 1992. *An Angel for Solomon Singer*. Ill. Peter Catalanotto. New York: Orchard.

Say, A. 2002. *Home of the Brave*. Boston, MA: Houghton Mifflin.

Sendak, M. 1963. *Where the Wild Things Are*. New York: HarperCollins.

Sis, P. 1996. *Starry Messenger*. New York: Frances Foster.

Thompson, C. 1998. *The Paradise Garden*. New York: Knopf.

Wagner, J. 1973. *The Bunyip of Berkeley's Creek*. Ill. Ron Wagner. Melbourne, Australia: Penguin Books.

Willard, N. 1991. *Pish, Posh, Said Hieronymus Bosch*. Ill. L. and D. Dillon. San Diego, CA: Harcourt Brace Jovanovich.

Van Allsburg, C. 1986. *The Stranger*. Boston, MA: Houghton Mifflin.

Appendix F
Frank's Current Top 25 Favorite Chapter Books

Avi. 1988. *Something Upstairs*. New York: Avon Books.

Babbit, N. 1969. *The Search for Delicious*. New York: HarperTrophy.

Babbit, N. 1975. *Tuck Everlasting*. New York: Farrar, Straus & Giroux.

Clements, A. 1996. *Frindle*. New York: Aladdin.

Cooper, S. 1993. *The Boggart*. New York: Macmillan McElderry.

Creech, S. 2001. *Love That Dog*. New York: HarperCollins.

Curtis, C. P. 1999. *Bud, Not Buddy*. New York: Delacorte Press.

Fleischman, S. 1986. *The Whipping Boy*. New York: Troll
    Communications L.L.C.

Fletcher, R. 1998. *Flying Solo*. New York: Dell Yearling.

Haddix, M. P. 1995. *Running Out of Time*. New York: Simon & Schuster.

Henkes, K. 1992. *Words of Stone*. New York: Greenwillow.

Juster, N. 1961. *The Phantom Tollbooth*. New York: Random House.

MacLachlan, P. 1991. *Journey*. New York: Dell.

Paterson, K. 1978. *The Great Gilly Hopkins*. New York: Harper & Row.

Paulson, G. 1995. *Nightjohn*. New York: Doubleday.

Peck, R. 2000. *A Year Down Yonder*. New York: Scholastic.

Rylant, C. 1995. *The Van Gogh Café*. New York: Scholastic.

Rylant, C. 1998. *The Islander*. New York: DK.

Spinelli, J. 1996. *Crash*. New York: Dell Yearling.

Spinelli, J. 2000. *Stargirl*. New York: Knopf.

Steig, W. 1972. *Dominic*. New York: Farrar, Straus & Giroux.

Steig, W. 1976. *Abel's Island*. New York: Farrar, Straus & Giroux.

Taylor, M. 1987. *The Friendship and the Gold Cadillac*. New York: Bantam.

Weik, M. H. 1966. *The Jazz Man*. New York: Macmillan.

Wojciechowska, M. 1964. *Shadow of a Bull*. New York: Macmillan.

Appendix G
Cyndi's Current Top 25 Picture Book
Read Alouds

Anderson, M. T. 2001. *Handel: Who Knew What He Liked*. Ill. K. Hawkes. Cambridge, MA: Candlewick.

Baylor, B. 1986. *I'm in Charge of Celebrations*. Ill. P. Parnall. New York: Simon & Schuster.

Best, C. 2001. *Shrinking Violet*. Ill. G. Potter. New York: Farrar, Straus & Giroux.

Burleigh, R. 1998. *Home Run*. Ill. M. Wimmer. San Diego, CA: Silver Whistle Harcourt Brace.

Chandra, D., and M. Comora. 2003. *George Washington's Teeth*. Ill. B. Cole. New York: Farrar, Straus & Giroux.

Cooney, B. 1982. *Miss Rumphius*. New York: Viking.

Cronin, D., 2000. *Click, Clack, Moo: Cows That Type*. Ill. B. Lewin. New York: Simon & Schuster.

Curlee, L. 1999. *Rushmore: Monument for the Ages*. New York: Scholastic.

DeFelice, C., and M. DeMarsh. 1995. *Three Perfect Peaches: A French Folktale*. Ill. I. Trivas. New York: Orchard.

George, K. O. 2002. *Swimming Upstream: Middle School Poems*. Ill. D. Tilley. New York: Clarion.

Hurst, C. O. 2001. *Rocks in His Head*. Ill. J. Stevenson. New York: Greenwillow.

Kerley, B. 2001. *The Dinosaurs of Waterhouse Hawkins*. Ill. B. Selznick. New York: Scholastic.

LaMarche, J. 2000. *The Raft*. New York: HarperCollins.

L'Engle, M. 2001. *The Other Dog*. New York: SeaStar.

Lester, J. 1994. *John Henry*. Ill. J. Pinkney. New York: Dial.

Lorbiecki, M. 1998. *Sister Anne's Hands*. Ill. W. Popp. New York: Dial Books.

Macaulay, D. 2002. *Angelo*. Boston, MA: Houghton Mifflin.

Marcus, L. 2002. *Side by Side: Five Favorite Picture-Book Teams Go to Work*. New York: Walker.

Nye, N. S. 2000. *Come with Me: Poems for a Journey*. Ill. D. Yaccarino. New York: Greenwillow.

Rappaport, D., and L. Callan. 2000. *Dirt on Their Skirts: The Story of the Young Women Who Won the World Championship*. Ill. E. B. Lewis. New York: Dial.

Ryan, P. M. 1999. *Amelia and Eleanor Go for a Ride*. Ill. B. Selznick. New York: Scholastic.

Ryan, P. M. 2002. *When Marian Sang*. Ill. by B. Selznick. New York: Scholastic.

Rylant, C. 1992. *An Angel for Solomon Singer*. Ill. P. Catalanotto. New York: Orchard.

Schroeder, A. 1997. *Smoky Mountain Rose: An Appalachia Cinderella*. Ill. B. Sneed. New York: Dial.

Thayer, E. L. 2000. *Casey at the Bat: A Ballad of the Republic Sung in the Year 1888*. Ill. C. Bing. Brooklyn, New York: Handprint Books.

Appendix H
Cyndi's Current Top 25 Chapter Book Read Alouds

Avi. 1999. *Midnight Magic*. New York: Scholastic.

Creech, S. 2001. *Love That Dog*. New York: HarperCollins.

Creech, S. 2002. *Ruby Holler*. New York: HarperCollins.

Curtis, C. P. 1999. *Bud, Not Buddy*. New York: Delacorte Press.

Cushman, K. 2000. *Matilda's Bone*. New York: Clarion.

DeCamillo, K. 2000. *Because of Winn-Dixie*. Cambridge, MA: Candlewick.

Ehrlich, A., ed. 1999. *When I Was Your Age: Original Stories About Growing Up Volume 1*. Cambridge, MA: Candlewick.

Fleischman, P. 1997. *Seedfolks*. New York: HarperCollins.

Freedman, R. 1987. *Lincoln: A Photobiography*. Boston: Houghton Mifflin.

Giff, P. R. 2000. *Nory Ryan's Song*. New York: Bantam Doubleday Dell.

Greenberg, J., and S. Jordan. 2001. *Frank O. Gehry: Outside In*. New York: DK Ink.

Haddix, M. P. 1999. *Just Ella*. New York: Simon & Schuster.

Hesse, K. 1997. *Out of the Dust*. New York: Scholastic.

Hiaasen, C. 2002. *Hoot*. New York: Knopf.

Hobbs, W. 1999. *Jason's Gold*. New York: Morrow.

Holt, K. W. 1998. *My Louisiana Sky*. New York: Holt.

Horvath, P. 2001. *Everything on a Waffle*. New York: Farrar, Straus & Giroux.

Jones, J. B. 2000. *Dear Mrs. Ryan, You're Ruining My Life*. New York: Walker.

Naylor, P. R. 1991. *Shiloh*. New York: Atheneum.

Peck, R. 1998. *A Long Way from Chicago*. New York: Dial.

Ryan, P. M. 2000. *Esperanza Rising*. New York: Scholastic.

Sachar, L. 1998. *Holes*. New York: Farrar, Straus & Giroux.

Snicket, L. *Series of Unfortunate Events* Series. New York: HarperCollins.

Wells, R. 1999. *Mary on Horseback: Three Mountain Stories*. New York: Viking.

Wiles, D. 2001. *Love, Ruby Lavender*. San Diego, CA: Harcourt.

Professional References

Anderson, R., E. Hiebert, J. Scott, and I. Wilkinson. 1985. *Becoming a Nation of Readers*. Washington, DC: National Institute of Education.

Bang, M. 2000. *Picture This: How Pictures Work*. New York: SeaStar.

Cummins, J. 1992. *Children's Book Illustration and Design*. New York: PBC International.

Darigan, D., M. Tunnel, and J. Jacobs. 2002. *Children's Literature*. New York: Prentice-Hall.

DePaola, T. 1987. Foreword to *Children's Literature in the Reading Program*, by Bernice E. Cullinan. Newark, DE: IRA.

Dewey, J. 1910. *How We Think*. Lexington, MA: D.C. Heath.

———. 1938. *Experience and Education*. New York: Simon & Schuster.

Fish, S. 1980. *Is There a Text in This Class? The Authority of Interpretive Communities*. Cambridge, MA: Harvard University Press.

Hancock, M. 2000. *A Celebration of Literature and Response*. Upper Saddle River, NJ: Prentice-Hall.

Heath, S. B. 1994. *Ways with Words: Language, Life and Work in Communities and Classrooms*. New York: Cambridge University Press.

Holdaway, D. 1979. *The Foundations of Literacy*. Portsmouth, NH: Heinemann.

Meek, M. 1988. *How Texts Teach Children to Read*. Gloucestershire, UK: Thimble Press.

Nodelman, P., and M. Neimer. 2003. *The Pleasures of Children's Literature*. 3rd edition. Boston: Allyn & Bacon.

Paterson, K. 1988. *The Gates of Excellence*. New York: Dutton Children's Books.

———. 1989. *The Spying Heart*. New York: Lodestar Books Dutton.

Pennac, D. 1999. *Better Than Life*. York, ME: Stenhouse.

Peterson, R. 1992. *Life in a Crowded Place*. Portsmouth, NH: Heinemann.

Peterson, R., and M. Eeds. 1990. *Grand Conversations: Literature Groups in Action*. New York: Scholastic.

Purves, A., and V. Rippere. 1968. *Elements of Writing About a Literary Work: A Study of Responses to Literature*. Urbana, IL: National Council of Teachers of English.

Rosenblatt, L. 1978. *The Reader, the Text, the Poem: The Transactional Theory of Literary Work*. Carbondale, IL: MLA.

Serafini, F. 2001. *The Reading Workshop: Creating Space for Readers*. Portsmouth, NH: Heinemann.

Sebesta, S., D. Monson, and H. D. Senn. 1995. "A Hierarchy to Assess Reader Response." *Journal of Reading* 38 (6): 444–50.

Sipe, L. 1998. "How Picture Books Work: A Semiotically Framed Theory of Text-Picture Relationships." *Journal of Children's Literature* 23: 6–19.

Vygotsky, L. 1962. *Thought and Language*. Cambridge, MA: MIT Press.

Williams, M. 1922. *The Velveteen Rabbit*. New York: Knopf.